Just Sentiments:
22 Smithian Essays

In March 2022, Adam Smith Works, a website of Liberty Fund, launched a new monthly feature called *Just Sentiments*. Collected here are the 22 essays that appeared during 2022–2023. Most are on the thought of Adam Smith, by scholars who study Smith. Each author draws on his or her own lengthier scholarly works, to offer interpretations that are important, textually grounded, and compactly expressed. The topics are: the polysemy of 'natural;' natural convention; jurisprudence, honest income, and the Great Enrichment; Smith's dual moral authorizations; David Hume on English liberty; Smith and Jamesian pragmatism; prudent entrepreneurship; words in and not in Smith's two masterpieces; the *History of Astronomy*; polygamy and kin networks; "By the Same Author"; poverty and liberty; moral judgment and governmentalization; the labor theory of value; Parmenides addresses Plato; French liberal economics 1695–1776; virtue and the court of princes; moral innovation and the man within the breast; Smith parries Philo on the problem of evil; Smith's endorsement of an interest-rate cap; Smith and Confucius; Smith on school funding.

Just Sentiments:
22 Smithian Essays

Edited by
Daniel B. Klein and Erik W. Matson

CL Press

Published by CL PRESS
A project of the Fraser Institute
1770 Burrard Street, 4th Floor
Vancouver, BC V6J 3G7 Canada
www.clpress.net

Just Sentiments: 22 Smithian Essays
Edited by Daniel B. Klein and Erik W. Matson

ISBN: 978-1-957698-15-1

Cover design by Jessica Hogenson
Interior layout by Joanna Andreasson

Searchable PDF of this book, with color in figures,
open access, free: https://clpress.net/

Contents

Preface & Acknowledgments

By Daniel B. Klein and Erik W. Matson

This volume collects the first 22 essays of the monthly feature launched in March 2022, *Just Sentiments*, which we edit for Liberty Fund for their wonderful website, *Adam Smith Works*. The 22 essays are presented here in the order in which they appeared. Authors have been invited to revise the essays but in all cases the essays have been revised only little or not at all.

In this book version, hyperlinks have been eliminated. Many of the figures originally contained links to the source of the data displayed in the figure. Readers may recur to the original essay at Adam Smith Works Just Sentiments to find such data sources.

The phrase "just sentiments" highlights the willful and cognitive aspect of sentiment, which is emphasized in Smith's ethics. The sentiment that someone experiences is influenced by actions he took prior to the experience. And, during the experience, or immediately after it, the person can reflect on his having felt the sentiment. He asks himself: Should I affirm the sentiment? Should I revise it? Should I reject it? The experiencing of a sentiment can be seen as a matter of the will and thus of acting justly. "Just sentiments" suggests one's responsibility for one's sentiments.

But the relationship between action and sentiment can also be turned around. "Just Sentiments" may suggest that sentiment causes action. Maybe a person's conduct is just sentiments. Maybe his learning, his reason, and his conclusions are just sentiments.

The relationship, then, seems to run in both directions—action to sentiment and sentiment to action. One could set up an action-sentiment spiral, for a journey that proceeds one loop to the next. Any sentiment can be asked: How do you justify your existence? And any action can be rendered as just an event in a history of sentiments.

Smith encourages us to actively shape our sentiments, through social interaction, education, sympathy with persons whom we look up to, and contemplation. Across his discourses he seeks to enhance and ennoble the sentiments of his readers. Even his social science may be seen in service to that end—for instance, his political economy instructs us toward juster sentiments on matters of public policy.

In *The Abolition of Man*, C.S. Lewis wrote: "The right defence against false sentiments is to inculcate just sentiments."

Acknowledgments: We are grateful to our friends and supporters at Liberty Fund, most especially Christy Horpedahl, who proofreads and formats the *Just Sentiments* essays as they appear at Adam Smith Works, offers final copy-edits, and generously handles all of the last-minute tweaking. We are grateful also to Amy Willis, Sarah Skwire, Douglas Den Uyl, of Liberty Fund, for their support of the *Just Sentiments* feature, and for permission to reproduce the material here. Kacey Reeves West helped to finalize the material as collected for publication in a single volume. The front-cover image on this book was designed by Jessica Hogenson and is used by permission of Liberty Fund. The interior was created by Joanna Andreasson.

Citing Smith's Works

(TMS 263.5) means page 263, paragraph 5 of *The Theory of Moral Sentiments*. Citations to Smith's works are to the Glasgow edition, published by Oxford University Press, and republished by Liberty Fund. The abbreviations are as follows:

TMS—*The Theory of Moral Sentiments*
WN—*The Wealth of Nations*
EPS—*Essays on Philosophical Subjects*
LJ—*Lectures on Jurisprudence*
LRBL—*Lectures on Rhetoric and Belles Lettres*
Corr.—*Correspondence of Adam Smith*

About the Authors

Jordan J. Ballor (Dr. theol., University of Zurich; Ph.D., Calvin Theological Seminary) is director of research at the Center for Religion, Culture & Democracy at First Liberty Institute. He is also associate director of the Junius Institute for Digital Reformation Research at Calvin Theological Seminary and the Henry Institute for the Study of Christianity & Politics at Calvin University and co-editor most recently of *Theology, Morality, and Adam Smith*.

Caroline Breashears is a Professor of English at St. Lawrence University.

Dylan DelliSanti is a writer and economist in Washington, D.C. In 2019 he defended his dissertation, "Three Essays on Adam Smith and the 'Corruption Debate,'" at George Mason University (Economics). He has taught at Northern Virginia Community College and the DC

Jail through the Georgetown University Prison Scholars Program. His research interests are in Adam Smith, intellectual history, and the ecology of cities.

Jonathon Diesel studied economics at George Mason University beginning in 2001 and culminating in a PhD in 2017. His research focuses on Adam Smith and expanding on Smithian concepts such as jural relationships and distinguishing the jural superior as a unique social role. He lives in northern Virginia with his family where he enjoys weekends watching his children grow. He is employed by a government contractor managing programs and providing systems engineering services.

Scott Drylie is an Assistant Professor of Economics, Cost Analysis, and Acquisition Management at the Air Force Institute of Technology in Dayton, Ohio. He earned his Ph.D. in Economics from George Mason University and holds an M.Ed. in Secondary Education. The views expressed in this paper are those of the author and do not reflect the official policy or position of the U.S. Air Force, the Department of Defense, or the U.S. government.

Patrick Fitzsimmons is a PhD student in economics at George Mason University, focusing on economic history. He is interested in early historical development and in the effects of informal and formal institutions on long-term development.

Jacob R. Hall is a Barry Postdoctoral Fellow at the University of Pennsylvania. He earned his Ph.D. in economics at George Mason University. His academic research is in economic history, economic growth, and political economy.

Andrew G. Humphries is a Visiting Assistant Professor of Economics at New College of Florida. He earned his Ph.D. in Economics from George Mason University, his M.Ed. in Education from Endicott College, and his B.A. in Liberal Arts from St. John's College, Santa Fe.

Daniel B. Klein is professor of economics and JIN Chair at the Mercatus Center at George Mason University. His books include *Central Notions of Smithian Liberalism* and *Smithian Morals*.

Benoît Malbranque, a research fellow at Institut Coppet, is studying French classical liberalism. He is the author of *Les théoriciens français de la liberté humaine* (Institut Coppet, 2020). He is currently working on a multi-volume encyclopedia of French classical liberalism.

Christopher Martin is an associate professor of economics at Hillsdale College in Michigan. He is a 2012 graduate of George Mason University's doctoral economics program

Erik Matson is a senior research fellow at the Mercatus Center at George Mason University and the deputy director of the GMU Adam Smith program.

Paul Mueller is a Senior Research Fellow at the American Institute for Economic Research and a Research Fellow at the Center for Culture, Religion, and Democracy where he is the Associate Director for the Religious Liberty in the States project. He received his PhD in economics from George Mason University and taught at The King's College in New York City. He is the author of *Ten Years Later: Why the Conventional Wisdom about the 2008 Financial Crisis is Still Wrong.*

Jon Murphy is an assistant professor of economics at Nicholls State University and Fellow at the Institute for an Entrepreneurial Society at Syracuse University. Dr. Murphy holds a Ph.D. in economics from George Mason University. His research interests include history of thought, economics of information, market failure, and law & economics.

Caleb Petitt is a third-year PhD student in economics at GMU and a F.A. Hayek fellow at the Mercatus Center. His research interests include Smithian political economy, public choice, and historical political economy.

John Robinson is an assistant professor of Intelligence Analysis at James Madison University. His research interests include the history of economic thought, institutional economics, and the philosophy of social science.

Paolo Santori is Assistant Professor of Philosophy at Tilburg University. His research interests include the history of economic thought, theology, and business ethics. Recently, he has been studying the philosophical and theological roots of the so-called three economic Enlightenments, i.e., the economic ideas of Adam Smith (Scottish Enlightenment), Immanuel Kant (German Enlightenment), and Antonio Genovesi (Italian Enlightenment).

Marcus Shera is a PhD student in Economics at George Mason University where he studies economic history of religion, and Smithian Political Economy. His research investigates the political economy of monasticism. He also writes and makes videos at theeconplayground.com.

J. Robert Subrick is an Associate Professor of Economics at James Madison University. His research focuses on southern African and Brazilian economic history with occasional forays into the history of economic thought.

Hairuo Tan is a fifth-year PhD student and graduate lecturer in economics at George Mason University. She received an M.S. in economics in 2018 from Trinity College, Dublin and a B.S. in Metallurgical and Materials Engineering in 2016 from Colorado School of Mines. Her dissertation on Adam Smith compares Smith and Confucius and assesses the paternalistic element in Smith's moral and political philosophy.

Kacey Reeves West is a PhD student in the Department of Economics at George Mason University and a PhD Fellow at the Mercatus Center.

CHAPTER 1

What's Natural about Adam Smith's Natural Liberty?

Daniel B. Klein and Erik W. Matson

Abundantly does Adam Smith use "liberty" in *The Wealth of Nations* (WN). "Liberty" usually means "allowing every man to pursue his own interest his own way" (WN 664.3). Smith sometimes adds an adjective, as in "perfect liberty" or "general liberty."

And then there is "natural liberty," which appears ten times. Ten is not a huge number. In fact, there are more occurrences of "perfect liberty"—sixteen. But the occurrences of "natural liberty" are significant. Most famous are those in the penultimate paragraph of Book IV:

> All systems either of preference or of restraint, therefore, being thus completely taken away, the obvious and simple system of **natural liberty** establishes itself of its own accord. Every man, as long as he does not violate the laws of justice, is left perfectly free to pursue his own interest his own way, and to bring both his industry and capital into competition with those of any other man, or order of men. The sovereign is completely discharged from a duty, in the attempting to perform which he must always be exposed

to innumerable delusions, and for the proper performance of which no human wisdom or knowledge could ever be sufficient; the duty of superintending the industry of private people, and of directing it towards the employments most suitable to the interest of the society. According to the system of **natural liberty**, the sovereign has only three duties to attend to... (WN 687.51, boldface added)

Four occurrences of "natural liberty" come when Smith points out that in endorsing a restriction on banks against issuing small-denomination notes he is making an exception to the principle of natural liberty: "But those exertions of the natural liberty of a few individuals, which might endanger the security of the whole society, are, and ought to be, restrained by the laws of all governments; of the most free, as well as of the most despotical" (WN 324.94).

Another comes in his outburst against the Settlement Act: "To remove a man who has committed no misdemeanour from the parish where he chuses to reside, is an evident violation of natural liberty and justice" (WN 157.59). Another comes in a remark: "Both laws were evident violations of natural liberty, and therefore unjust" (WN 530.16). And two come when he says that repealing "encroachments upon natural liberty" would ease the readjustment of those put out of work by free trade (WN 470.42).

In all ten cases, "natural liberty" means the flipside to commutative justice. Commutative justice is not messing with others' person, property, and promises due, and the flipside is others—including the government—not messing with one's own such stuff. Smith pegs natural liberty as the flipside of commutative justice when he says "[b]oth laws were violations of natural liberty and *therefore* unjust" (WN 530.16, italics added). Smith often said simply "liberty" but sometimes "natural liberty."

Why did Smith sometimes say "natural liberty"? Maybe he wanted to highlight its "naturalness." That prompts the question: What is "natural" about Smith's "natural liberty"?

"Nature" and "natural" loom large in Smith. The words feature in the full titles of his two published works: *An Inquiry into the Nature and Causes of the Wealth of Nations* and *The Theory of Moral Sentiments, or An Essay towards an Analysis of the Principles by which Men naturally judge concerning the Conduct and Character, first of their Neighbours, and afterwards of themselves.* But the meaning of "nature" eludes simple definition. According to A.L. Macfie (1967), "Smith's 'Nature' is like Heinz's tins—there are fifty-seven varieties" (7).

The polysemy of "nature" and its cognates was well known. David Hume claimed there is no word "more ambiguous and unequivocal" than "nature" and offered three (among many) possible definitions: that which is opposed to miracles, that which is opposed to the rare and unusual, and that which is opposed to artifice (Hume 2007, 304–5). Samuel Johnson, in his *Dictionary of the English Language*, lists thirteen definitions of "nature", along with eight of "natural."

In TMS Smith sometimes plays different ideas of nature off one another, telling how "man is by Nature directed to correct, in some measure, that distribution of things which she herself would otherwise have made" (TMS 168.9). Our natural moral sentiments often lead us to strive against aspects of "nature," or the way things usually are in the world. Tyranny, domination, monopoly, and coercion are natural, and, naturally, we rail against them (cf. Brubaker 2006; Pack 1995).

Let's focus on "natural." Here are four definitions that advance a Smithian understanding:

1. Existing in the primeval human state, with only primitive language, the most basic forms of property, and

no subordination to a political body. Making a contrast with "artificial," which itself has multiple senses, Hume said: "Sucking is an action natural to Man, and Speech is artificial" (published in back matter of Hume 2007, 430).

2. Usual or expected as in "the natural and ordinary state of mankind" (TMS 45.7).

3. Necessary for the state of human affairs that the speaker presupposes or posits.

4. Worth naturalizing, which is to say, worth actualizing such that we get to a state of affairs in which the thing we say is natural would then be expected (sense 2) or necessary (sense 3).

There are yet other meanings of "natural" in Smith,[1] among which we could include:

a. essential or definitionally necessary;

b. resultant from human action but not human design, as in natural versus artificial (here we have a second sense of "artificial");

c. not resultant from actions of superior beings, as in natural versus supernatural.

Also, in WN we have "natural" price/wage/rent/rate/proportion/balance and so on. These sometimes relate to expected or necessary; also, sometimes, they might be thought of as outcomes obtaining under a certain set of hypothetical assumptions, as in an equilibrium model.

But put these other meanings aside, and let us continue with the enumerated four senses.

---

1. Charles Griswold (1999, 311–17) lists seven.

These four senses launch a dynamic. Evolution generated "man," in his primeval state, which might be associated with the end of the environment of evolutionary adaptedness, namely small bands at the end of the Paleolithic Age (10,000 BC). The primeval maps, in Smith, to the hunter stage of social development.

Once man—and hence man-in-society—has been posited, whether primeval or beyond, there operates a recursive dynamic of senses 2, 3, and 4. In the Neolithic Age, with agriculture and settlement, new practices and structures develop; new regularities in social life develop, and become expected and therefore natural (sense 2). People also become aware of different societies with different regularities, or of changes in their own society over time, and see that preconditions are necessary to arrive at and sustain certain social arrangements (sense 3).

Finally, a sense of the common good—in us since the primeval and natural in all four senses— looks to improvement; certain practices thought to advance the good are endorsed. They are thought to be potentialities that *ought to be actualized* (sense 4). Should they be actualized, they become natural in senses 2 and 3. Sense 4 is "natural" in its *becoming* sense.

With the four definitions in mind, we again ask: What's natural about Smith's natural liberty?

Even in the primeval state, we have ownership of our person and immediate possessions. David Friedman (1994, 14-15) affirms that we have "natural property" in our own person, by virtue of a special knowledge and control of it, and our mutual recognition of one another's spheres of knowledge and control. Bart Wilson argues similarly in *The Property Species: Mine, Yours, and the Human Mind* (2020), saying that "no human parents in any community have to teach their child to resist attempts to take things securely within their grasp. Children are natural-born possessors" (9). Wilson propounds the idea that we naturally "emphysicalize the concept of mine" (15), a concept that starts with the most personal of objects, our own mind and an our own body. Hume affirmed the special relationship we have in the "fix'd and constant advantages of the mind and body" (Hume 2007, 314).

Thus, there is self-ownership in the primeval state. Indeed, hunter-gatherer bands did not have the hierarchy and technology to enslave. A band that did not accord its members self-ownership simply would not survive. A band is best thought of as an association of jural equals. The vision is also true to Smith on the hunter stage.

When Smith then moves to the more advanced stages, of shepherds, of agriculture, and of commerce, he says that property is *extended* (LJ 10, 16, 19-23, 27, 34, 38, 39, 207, 308, 309, 432. 434, 460, 466, 467, 468). Property in one's own person is primevally natural, and the principle is subsequently extended to objects that in the primeval state had not yet been propertized.

Self-ownership, the core of "one's own" or *suum* in Latin, is thus natural in sense 1, and one's own is the basis for liberty, in the main sense in which Smith uses the term. So liberty has a good claim to being natural in sense 1. Now, can liberty claim to be natural in senses 2, 3, and 4?

Is liberty, in Smith's time and ours, usual or expected? Yes and no. We will come back to the "yes" in our next essay, but here we highlight the "no." Arbitrary political arrangements that yield economic and religious monopolies, burdensome tax schemes and regulations, restrictions on the freedom of movement and expression are the norm. We might say that the *unnaturalness* of liberty is presupposed by Smith's entire project. Why write a book like *The Wealth of Nations* if one believes liberty to be a natural tendency in political affairs? (See Brubaker 2006, 332.)

In his *Lectures on Jurisprudence*, which crib extensively from Hume's *History of England*, Smith tells of political development in England—which he reckoned the most liberal polity. In France and Spain, "the absolute power of the sovereigns has continu'd ever since its establishment...In England alone a different government has been established from the naturall course of things" (LJ 265). Against the natural course of things, Smith says, England didn't develop a large standing army; without a standing force, the sovereign had to assemble Parliament to go to war. English Parliament—the Commons in particular—asserted itself against the crown, leading, after great convulsions, to the shoring up of institutions supportive of individual liberty: the limit of royal prerogative, the firming up of the rule of law, the regularization of legal practice. For Smith and Hume, the existence of liberty in Britain, such as it was, was not usual or particularly expected.

The same feeling of the unnaturalness of liberty (in sense 2) runs through WN. Consider, again: "All systems either of preference or of restraint, therefore, being thus completely taken away, the obvious and simple system of natural liberty establishes itself of its own accord" (WN 687.51). Natural liberty does not simply establish itself of its own accord. Systems of preference and restraint flow ubiquitously from aspects of human nature: partiality, desire for public esteem, limited knowledge, and so on. It is within Smith's contemplation and judgment that systems of preference and restraint are taken away. Only then, and within such a vision, does the system of natural liberty emerge as obvious and simple.[1]

Natural liberty is natural because it is worth naturalizing. The system of natural liberty may be taken as "some general, and even systematical, idea of the perfection of policy and law" intended to direct "the views of the statesman" (TMS 234.18). Smith realizes that the expectation that liberty "should ever be entirely restored in Great Britain, is as absurd as to expect that an Oceana or Utopia should be established in it" (WN 471.43). But his work attempts to persuade British political practice into beliefs that will augment liberty. His

---

1. This paragraph draws from Brubaker (2006, 338).

posture is presumptively in favor of a policy reform that allows individuals greater degrees of freedom to pursue their interest, within the rules of justice, in their own way, although it is possible that Smith will make an exception to the general presumption.[1]

A presumption of liberty is worth naturalizing because it serves the good of humankind. Smith's economic analysis illustrates how commerce facilitates "the co-operation...of great multitudes" (WN 26.2). But the benefits of the market process depend upon liberty, the "liberal and generous system" (WN 671.24), not the "illiberal and oppressive" measures of mercantilism (WN 584.50).

Degrees of flourishing require degrees of liberalness in government policy. That shows how liberty is necessary and therefore may be said to be natural in sense 3. Although it is not a usual and expected feature of human history, some degree of liberty is necessary for the flourishing states of affairs described in WN, such as the "higgling and bargaining" dynamics of the price system (WN 49.4).

"Let the same natural liberty of exercising what species of industry they please be restored to all his majesty's subjects" (WN 470.42). Smith believes that the liberty of each individual *ought* to be honored, even though it can never be held inviolate, a liberty corresponding to the individual's society's conventions of self-ownership and property between jural equals. Smith believes that each *ought* to be dignified in liberty, the way of better living. Built on the natural property that each soul has in his or her person (sense 1), the goodness of liberty (sense 4) is the principal reason why natural liberty is natural.

We leave this chapter with a plan to continue on "natural." The next will consider "natural" versus "conventional," and suggest a concept, *natural convention*, which combines nature and convention.

---

1. This paragraph draws on Brubaker (2006, 338)

References

Brubaker, Lauren. 2006. Does the 'wisdom of Nature' Need Help? In *New Voices on Adam Smith*, ed. Leonidas Montes and Eric Schliesser, 330–72. New York: Routledge.

Friedman, David. 1994. A Positive Account of Property Rights. *Social Philosophy and Policy* 11(2): 1–16.

Griswold, Charles L. 1999. *Adam Smith and the Virtues of Enlightenment*. New York: Cambridge University Press.

Hume, David. 2007. *A Treatise of Human Nature*, eds. David F. Norton and Mary J. Norton. 2 vols. Oxford: Oxford University Press.

Macfie, A. L. 1967. The Moral Justification of Free Enterprise. *Scottish Journal of Political Economy* 14(1): 1–11.

Pack, Spencer J. 1995. Adam Smith's Unnaturally Natural (Nonetheless Naturally Unnatural) Use of the Word Natural. In *The Classical Tradition in Economic Thought: Perspectives on the History of Economic Thought: Vol. XI*, ed. Ingrid H. Rima, 31–42. Aldershot: Edward Elgar.

Smith, Adam. 1981. *An Inquiry into the Nature and Causes of the Wealth of Nations*, eds. R.H. Campbell and A.S. Skinner. 2 vols. Indianapolis: Liberty Fund.

Smith, Adam. 1982a. *Lectures on Jurisprudence*, eds. R.L. Meek, D.D. Raphael, and P.G. Stein. Indianapolis: Liberty Fund.

Smith, Adam. 1982b. *The Theory of Moral Sentiments*, eds. D.D. Raphael and A.L. Macfie. Indianapolis: Liberty Fund.

Wilson, Bart J. 2020. *The Property Species: Mine, Yours, and the Human Mind*. New York: Oxford University Press.

CHAPTER 2

Nature, Convention, and Natural Convention

Daniel B. Klein and Erik W. Matson

I n Chapter 1 we said that liberty is natural in important senses of the term. We also said that liberty is a flipside of commutative justice. (CJ = commutative justice.)

Given that Smith is closely associated with David Hume, one may ask: How does all the naturalness square with a famous statement in *A Treatise of Human Nature*, published 1740? Hume said that a sense of CJ "is not deriv'd from nature, but arises artificially" ([1740], 311).

Smith's account of justice differs slightly from Hume's. He more emphasizes the role of resentment and regards "utility" as a matter of secondary importance. (We treat the matter in Matson, Doran, and Klein 2019.) But whatever the daylight between them, Hume's distinction between natural and artificial still helps us think about ways in which liberty is and isn't natural for Smith. If CJ is artificial, and "not deriv'd from nature," how can we lavish liberty with naturalness?

Some of the most important words in Hume and Smith are polysemes. A contrariety might arise because one sentences uses the polyseme in one sense while another uses it in another. Hume and Smith both played with *nature* and *natural*. Other polysemes include *reason* and *liberty* in Hume and justice and *impartial spectator* in Smith.

Also, in 1775 Hume disavowed the *Treatise* (Klein 2017). That doesn't mean that we should disregard what Hume called his "juvenile work," but it does mean that if a statement in the *Treatise* conflicts with his thought generally and does not find life in his subsequent writings, it is reasonable to consider whether it was an act of juvenile indiscretion. That applies here, for in his subsequent writings the only mention of CJ as artificial comes in a footnote in an appendix to enquiry on morals, a footnote that obliterates the claim (Hume [1751], 99).

Moreover, in the *Treatise* itself Hume walked back the notion that justice is not natural. He accords justice a place among the "laws of nature" because it is "obvious and absolutely" necessity for social life. "Hume's aim," Stephen Buckle (1991, 298) writes, "is not to replace natural law, but to complete it." In a similar vein Knud Haakonssen (1981, 12) writes that Hume combined "the strands of his inheritance into a completely new sort of natural law theory – for, indeed, he is quite willing to use that label, provided we let him fill in the contents himself."

What is Hume's "new sort of natural law theory"? The theory flows out of Hume's notion of convention, a word often set in opposition to nature. Expositing Humean convention helps us transcend the opposition and propose "natural convention." The idea of natural convention illumines liberty's naturalness.

There is no such thing as the only possible convention

It is a convention among English speakers to call the thing we normally sip coffee from a "cup." Meanwhile, among Swedes the convention is "kopp."

One of the key elements that make the regularity of saying "cup" a convention is that there is an alternative possible regularity, such as "kopp," which, too, would satisfy the other elements making a convention among English speakers. If "kopp" were the regularity among English speakers, some English speaker John would say "kopp," and he would want each of the other English speakers to say "kopp." As David K. Lewis (1969, 70) put it, "there is no such thing as the only possible convention."

We could say "kopp," but we happen to say "cup." The important thing is that we are "on the same page"—that expression implies that there are other possible pages on which could mutually coordinate. Thus, convention carries a connotation of adventitious, inessential, or even arbitrary—"Which page shall we pick up at?" That which is conventional did not arise by necessity. It was not dictated by nature.

However, isn't it usual, expected, and beneficial, even necessary in some respects, that an American, among Americans, say "cup"? Isn't it *natural* for Americans to say "cup"?

Consider the following deeper regularity: *That one raised up in a language community, or long integrated into it, speak the language of that community.* Upon that deeper regularity it follows, given the semantics of the two languages, that Americans say "cup" and Swedes say "kopp."

Now, is that deeper regularity, too, a convention? No, it is not. There is not an alternative regularity that, too, would satisfy the other elements making convention. Indeed, it is unclear what that other regularity would even be. But if you imagine one, realize that it has to satisfy other conditions for convention, notably: under general adhesion to the regularity, John's conforming to it is good for John, and each other person's conforming to it is good for John. There is no such alternative regularity. Thus, we lack warrant for calling the deeper regularity conventional. Recall Lewis's words: There is no such thing as the only possible convention. Hence, that deeper regularity is *not* a convention.

It is apt to call that deeper regularity natural. It is usual, expected, and beneficial, even necessary in some respects, on a wider plane of human experience. Underneath that which is conventional ("cup" rather than "kopp") we can often find a deeper and more abstract behavioral regularity, even spanning countries and epochs, that is not conventional but rather natural.

We said that in the *Treatise* Hume walked back CJ as artificial. Here is the most notable passage:

> To avoid giving offence [Ha!], I must here observe, that when I deny justice to be a natural virtue, I make use of the word, *natural*, only as oppos'd to *artificial*. In another sense of the word; as no principle of the human mind is more natural than a sense of virtue; so no virtue is more natural than justice. Mankind is an inventive species; and where an invention is obvious and absolutely necessary, it may as properly be said to be natural as any thing that proceeds immediately from original principles, without the intervention of thought or reflexion. Tho' the rules of justice be *artificial*, they are not *arbitrary*. Nor is the expression improper to call them *Laws of Nature*; if by natural we understand what is common to any species, or even if we confine it to mean what is inseparable from the species. (Hume [1740], 311)

In fact, winks of CJ as natural come in many spots in the wake of Hume's declaration that it is artificial. (See: "nature provides a remedy," "nature must furnish the materials," "this progress of sentiments be *natural*," "and also by the laws of nature," "invention of the law of nature," "three fundamental laws of nature," "observance of these rules follows naturally.") Remember what Hume's *Treatise* is a treatise of.

If, underneath the surface, the rules of CJ are natural, in what sense are they "artificial"? In what sense are they conventional?

CJ as conventional

Chapter 1 said that, by the special knowledge and control that each soul has over its person, David Friedman (1994) proposed that your person is your "natural property," and we may add immediate possessions. And we said that would go even in the primeval state, and that Hume said as much in speaking of the special relation we have with our mind and body. Property implies ownership, a norm bearing on others not to mess.

For society to advance, objects not yet propertized in the primeval state need to be propertized. People, Hume said,

> must seek for a remedy, by putting these goods, as far as possible, on the same footing with the fix'd and constant advantages of the mind and body. This can be done after no other manner, than by a **convention** enter'd into by all the members of the society to bestow stability on the possession of those external goods, and leave every one in the peaceable enjoyment of what he may acquire by his fortune and industry. (Hume [1740], 314)

Understand that "a convention enter'd into" does not imply contract. Hume immediately says: "This convention is not of the nature of a *promise*." Hume used the word *convention* in an innovative way that would eventually find definitive exposition in Lewis's book *Convention; A Philosophical Study* (1969). (We discuss Hume's innovation in "Convention without Convening," Matson and Klein 2022.)

Not everything that is agreeable arises from contractual agreement. A lovely spring day is agreeable, but did not arise from agreement. Likewise, when two men "pull the oars of a boat," they find a mutually coordinated pace "tho' they have never given promises to each other" ([1740], 315). "In like manner are languages gradually establish'd by human conventions without any promise. In like manner do gold and silver become the common measures of exchange" ([1740], 315).

By "artificial," Hume means post-primeval. He speaks of man "in *uncultivated nature*" and "in his rude and more natural condition". Note how those phrasings allow *cultivated* nature and man's *less-but-still* natural condition. Again, according to Hume and Smith, the basic principle of ownership gets *extended*. It is those extensions, beyond the primeval state, that Hume is calling artificial.

The basic precept of CJ is: Don't mess with other people's stuff. But what counts as "stuff"? Say it is England in the year 1400. And what makes the stuff one person's rather than another's, or no one's? And what counts as "messing with" it? Answers to those questions were filled in by particular rules operative in that time and place. Those rules—among jural equals—provided the social grammar of that time and place, just as Middle English provided a linguistic grammar. These answers were conventional, even if they bore close resemblance to conventions of other times or places. But conventions do change somewhat. Have you ever tried reading Middle English?

Consider testamentary succession in England in 1400. Suppose a family proposed to disregard entailments on its lands, which restrict to whom the property can pass. Would that be a violation of CJ? Would it be messing with someone's stuff? CJ rules as regards testamentary specifications have varied over time, with convention. For conventions as between two different contexts, it is sometimes foolish to think that one was right while the other was wrong, just as it would be foolish to say that Americans are right to say "cup" and Swedes wrong to say "kopp."

Or jump much further back in time, to 10,000 BC: Smith says that land itself was not propertized until the third stage of social development, agriculture. Whether what one did with land was in line with CJ would depend on certain conventions of time and place.

CJ as natural

CJ's basic precept—Don't mess with other people's stuff—which we should understand firstly in the jural relationship between jural equals, like you and your neighbor—is a general principle, and many of its specifics must be filled in by the conventions of time and place. Systems of CJ vary somewhat by time and place.

But there is uniformity amidst variety. Whatever time and place we speak of, the society won't fare well if neighbors mess with each other's stuff. Smith said that a basic regard for CJ's precept is "indispensable." Hume said that without such regard "society must immediately dissolve." Thus, if we speak of society, there must be some basic regard for shared understandings of CJ. That uniformity spells natural: usual, expected, necessary for the state of social existence supposed in discourse, and beneficial. Even in the primeval state, fellow members of the Paleolithic band presumably did not much mess with one another's stuff.

CJ as natural convention

We can define natural convention as a social practice whose concrete form in time and place allows for various expressions (and is therefore conventional), but whose generalized form is necessary (and hence natural) to social development beyond the primeval state.

CJ is a prime example of a natural convention. Other examples include political authority and language. There are (and have been) myriad understandings of what, exactly, constitutes property and how that cashes out in social and legal practice. Those myriad understandings give rise to corresponding notions about property violations. But, throughout, is the idea that property is not to be violated; *in every community*, violations of property give rise to the passion of resentment. The community's manifestations of CJ are distinctive in many respects, and adherence to those conventions is mutually agreeable. But the general form of CJ, across communities, is natural. There is uniformity amidst variety.

In *The Fatal Conceit* (p. 17), Friedrich Hayek provides an analogy: "There may exist just one way to satisfy certain requirements for forming an extended order – just as the development of wings is apparently the only way in which organisms can become able to fly (the wings of insects, birds, and bats have quite different genetic origins)." Wings are the only way for organisms to fly, even though in nature we see many different types of wings. So too are extended notions of CJ the only way for a society to advance beyond the primeval, even though we see different conventions of CJ.

Liberty as natural convention

In Chapter 1 we noted ways in which liberty is not usual or expected. Now, we highlight ways in which it is, and therefore in those senses natural.

Again, liberty, in the way that Smith's WN primarily uses the word, is a flipside of CJ, and CJ is necessary to any sustainable community. In Chapter 1, we saw how Smith saw that the principle of ownership was extended outward, beginning with self-ownership, to other objects; thus various objects are brought within emergent rules of CJ, rules that are grammar-like, that is, "precise and accurate," as Smith puts it (TMS 327.1). Smith indicates a naturalness to the extending of ownership: "In some countries, the rudeness and barbarism of the people hinder the natural sentiments of justice from arriving at that accuracy and precision which, in more civilized nations, they *naturally* attain to" (TMS 341.36, italics added).

An evolved, refined CJ paves the way to the spirit of liberty. In a modern nation-state, neighbors generally refrain from messing with each other's stuff. As for the governor-governed jural relationship, the government institutionalizes its "messings," in the form of taxation and myriad restrictions. In any time and place, CJ conceptually pins down the contours of liberty in that setting, on the following principle: *An action taken by government is an initiation of coercion if and only if such action if taken by a neighbor or other jural equal would be an initiation of coercion.*

Thus, as long as CJ is alive among neighbors, liberty naturally exists as a concept. Like CJ, the specific contours of liberty vary somewhat with time and place. But we can pin down those contours by consulting the conventions of CJ among jural equals in that time and place. Smith's expressions associated with liberty—for example, "of their own accord," "allowing every man to pursue his own interest his own way"—become substantively meaningful as pinned down by the principle stated in the preceding paragraph.

And liberty usually spells prosperity. Societies with liberal policies, therefore, grow rich and come to have outsized military, political, cultural, and economic influence. Thus, there is some basis to expect liberal tendencies. Something usual or expected is in that sense natural.

And, as we said previously, liberal policy is generally beneficial for the whole, and in that sense, too, natural. A presumption of liberty is worth naturalizing. It is proper to instill attachments to a presumption of liberty.

To sum up:

1. Liberty has a conceptual dual in CJ.

2. CJ begins, even in the primeval band, with the soul's ownership of its person, and history then extends the principle of ownership to other objects.

3. CJ is natural although particulars vary, as with wings among species of flying organisms.

4. As CJ is pinned down, substantively, in time and place, so too is liberty.

5. Liberty presents itself as a coherent principle of nature. Tyrants will battle against liberty but they cannot destroy it as a living idea without destroying society.

Liberal civilization, which is only several centuries old, is a newcomer to the pageant of human history. But the principles of individual self-ownership and equal, rule-of-law subjection under government, and a presumption of liberty bearing on government, can be called natural conventions—if only for the subpopulation cherishing those principles—of a natural development in the story of humankind.

References

Buckle, Stephen. 1991. *Natural Law and the Theory of Property: Grotius to Hume.* Clarendon Press.

Friedman, David. 1994. A Positive Account of Property Rights. *Social Philosophy and Policy* 11 (2): 1–16.

Haakonssen, Knud. 1981. *The Science of a Legislator: The Natural Jurisprudence of David Hume and Adam Smith.* Cambridge University Press.

Hayek, Friedrich A. 1988. *The Fatal Conceit: The Errors of Socialism.* University of Chicago Press.

Hume, David. 2007 [1740]. *A Treatise of Human Nature*, edited by D. F. Norton and M. J. Norton. 2 vols. Oxford University Press.

Hume, David. 1998 [1751]. *An Enquiry Concerning the Principles of Morals*, edited by T. L. Beauchamp. Clarendon Press.

Klein, Daniel B. 2017. Glimpses of David Hume. *Econ Journal Watch* 14 (3): 474–487.

Lewis, David K. 1969. *Convention: A Philosophical Study.* Cambridge, MA: Harvard University Press.

Matson, Erik W., Colin Doran, and Daniel B. Klein. 2019. Hume and Smith on Utility, Agreeableness, Propriety, and Moral Approval. *History of European Ideas* 45 (5): 675–704.

Matson, Erik W., and Daniel B. Klein. 2022. Convention without Convening: Hume's Marvelous Innovation. *Constitutional Political Economy* 33 (1): 1–24.

Smith, Adam. 1982b. *The Theory of Moral Sentiments*, eds. D.D. Raphael and A.L. Macfie. Indianapolis: Liberty Fund.

CHAPTER 3

McCloskey's Narrative and Jurisprudence

Daniel B. Klein

Deirdre McCloskey awakens us to the Great Enrichment commencing a decade or two after *The Wealth of Nations* in 1776. Her bourgeois trilogy (McCloskey 2006; 2010; 2016) and other books (McCloskey 2019; McCloskey and Carden 2020) treat the causes. It is a story of growing openness during the 17th and 18th centuries to 'having a go.'

Liberal sentiments and ideas were communicated by speech and print. Persuasion and edification came by intellectual and moral leadership. The paramount figure was and is Adam Smith. He morally authorized your having a go, and morally authorized *allowing others* to have a go—liberalization. Adam Smith called it "allowing every man to pursue his own interest his own way" (WN 664.3). McCloskey's story is the lead-up to that cresting of cultural leadership and the resultant enrichment.

McCloskey's narrative is worth enhancing. I accentuate the role of jurisprudence, about which McCloskey says only a little. We can understand how crucial jurisprudence was historically only by understanding how crucial it is conceptually.

Ngrams bolster McCloskey's narrative

Below is a diagram of five ngrams—four 2grams and one 3gram. One of the 2grams is "virtuous industry," charted by the dark blue line. The vertical axis is the percentage of all gazillion 2grams in millions of books that are "virtuous industry."

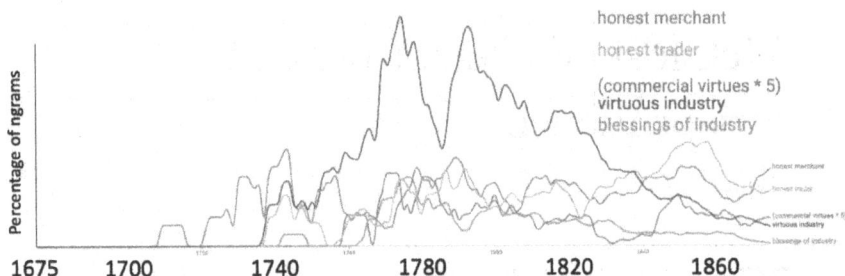

The striking thing about the figure is the flatline from 1675 to about 1740 for most of the ngrams shown. "Virtuous industry" was zilch—zilch!—from 1675 to 1736, and then some people started writing "virtuous industry." Virtue + industry, what a notion!

It's similar for "honest trader," "blessings of industry," "honest merchant," and "commercial virtues." The last one I've multiplied by 5 to make it visible with the others. All of the lines were zilch and then come into being. McCloskey says that commerce and industry became honored. Formerly regarded as lacking in virtue, commerce and industry became respectable, even virtuous. The lines beautifully illustrate what she says.

Likewise, "fair profits" and "honest profits" prove that McCloskey is right: Around 1770 some people started to talk of "fair profits" and "honest profits." Profits could be fair and honest—who knew?!

In *Bourgeois Equality* (2016, ch. 25), McCloskey says that the word *honest* underwent profound change. In Shakespeare's time, honest meant noble, aristocratic, loyal, honorable. By Smith's time, it had

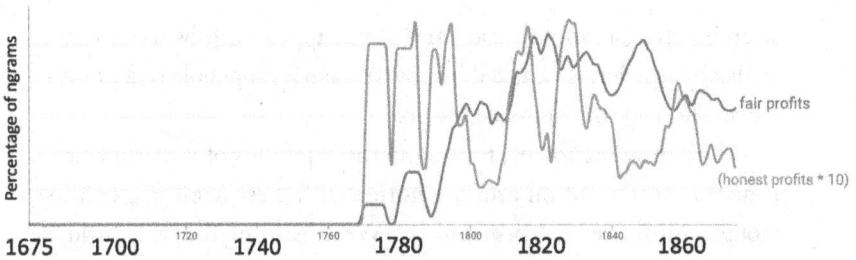

shifted to how we think of it—truthful, upright—and for all. McCloskey demonstrates the change, and that "an identical shift occurs in non-English Germanic languages" (2016, 247). To illustrate, she quotes TMS: "The poor man must neither defraud nor steal from the rich.... There is no commonly honest man who does not more dread the inward disgrace of such an action" (TMS 138.6). McCloskey writes: "In Shakespeare 'commonly honest' would commonly be an honest contradiction in terms and 'honest but poor' an absurdity" (2016, 240).

In the ngram figures above, look at the "honest" lines: Before the eighteenth century, "honest merchant," "honest trader," "honest profits" are zero. The figures confirm McCloskey's narrative.

After Adam Smith, Tocqueville's America of the 1830s largely subscribed to the new gospel: "In the United States professions are more less onerous, more or less lucrative, but they are never high or low. Every honest profession is honorable" (Tocqueville [1840], 526).

Having a go — But at what?

Again, McCloskey's story is about Smith and others morally authorizing your having a go, and morally deauthorizing your preventing others from having a go. But a go at what?

Back in the old traditional society, there was more of a status or station in carving stone for hire or baking bread for sale. Vocations more often involved a sanctification and social approval. Jobs were boxed in also by restrictions backed by government, and people had not yet learned how to think outside the box.

With growing towns, trade, and the teachings of jurisprudence, a more abstract notion arose, a notion of honest dealings. It is as though cultural leaders began to say: We're learning that the world is too darned complicated to pretend to know, and we will pretend no longer to track the particulars of time and place. As long as you don't mess with anyone's stuff, have a go and we'll recognize the pecuniary residuals as fair profits. Earnings. Honest income.

But are people to win a livelihood at prostitution and salacious arts? And what about blasphemy? Sedition, treason, and pernicious moral and political literature?

Many a menace to liberal civilization got rich through the honest dealings involved in writing and publishing books. Having a go may be conducted to honest profit, but such profiting may not be virtuous. A tension surrounds the problem of profiting that is honest but not virtuous. That is but one of the quandaries of liberalism.

Fortunately, the arc of liberalism grappled with the paradoxes and continued upward. A key was to clarify honest as distinct from virtuous. Justice had layers. In equal-equal relationships, honest was, in effect, advanced as a necessary but not sufficient condition for virtuous. A conceptualization of honest—or *just*, in a basic, mere sense, clarified by jural theorists—came forward. The conceptualization opened up new ways of seeing things, and sparked the imagination. People were allowed and even encouraged to think outside the box. The result was *innovation*, the electrical spark in the engine of enrichment.

Consider the rise of "earnings" and "income":

Both "earnings" and "income" pick up after 1740. Think about what "earnings" means. It means what you net from your honest commerce, whether you sell goods or services. Never mind what goods or

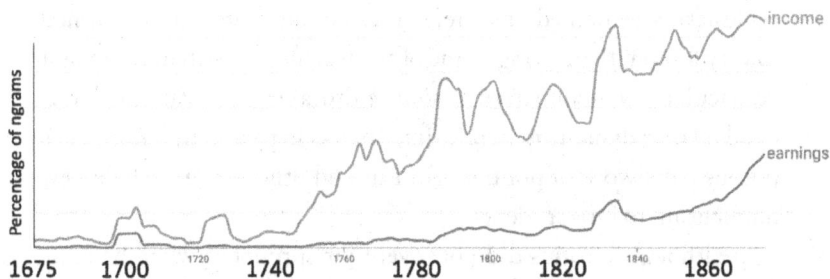

services. It's really quite abstract. Earnings are what you have from your honest dealings, whatever those dealings might be.

Jurisprudence, the printing press, the vernacular, literacy, and press dynamism

Scholars like Brian Tierney (1997, 2014) have explained that notions of permissive, open-ended individual rights start up significantly in the 12th century, and a steady stream flows into the Dutchman Hugo Grotius. Moreover, the Romans had developed jurisprudence. In a sketch of European history, Hume wrote:

> [P]erhaps there was no event, which tended farther to the improvement of the age, than one, which has not been much remarked, the accidental finding of a copy of Justinian's Pandects, about the year 1130, in the town of Amalfi in Italy. The ecclesiastics, who had leisure, and some inclination of study, immediately adopted with zeal this excellent system of jurisprudence, and spread the knowledge of it throughout every part of Europe. (Hume 1983 II, 520)

However, prior to the printing press, such teachings of zealous ecclesiastics remained obscure, contested, disjointed, and confined to very few. With printing, some of the teachings—still in Latin, not vernacular—were imparted to some cultural leaders. Europe developed relative dynamism in printing, thanks in part to the continent's porous patchwork of polities. Grotius and others give a whole new momentum to jurisprudence.

Although Grotius did not invent jurisprudence when he published the three-volume *The Rights of War and Peace* in 1625, it is a major development. In 1839 Henry Hallam wrote: "It is acknowledged by every one, that the publication of this treatise made an epoch in the philosophical, and almost, we might say, the political history of Europe" (1839, 181).

Spurred in part by the Protestant emphasis on a direct and personal connection with God and hence scripture, literacy was taking root. But it was slow to expand. Only in the vernacular and with rising print-culture could ideas be propounded to that emergent entity called "the people" or "the public."

When it came to works in jurisprudence, a Briton's ability to read English might not even be good enough, as in the earlier part of 18th century, some of the important works were still composed in Latin, including ones by the Glasgow professors Gershom Carmichael and Francis Hutcheson. In Britain, jurisprudence comes to be written and taught *in the English language* only in the 18th century. Thus, from 1675 to the 1740s, the English word *jurisprudence* was little used. Nonethe-

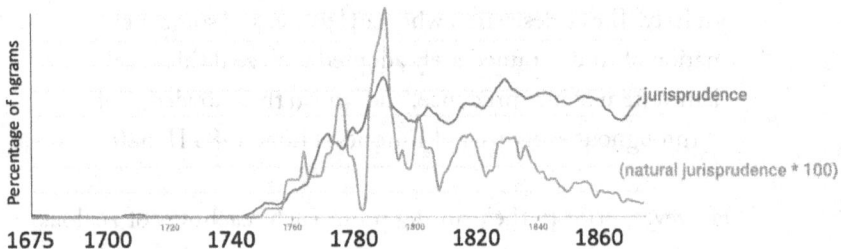

less, jurisprudential teachings were important for Latinate cultural leaders like Carmichael and Hutcheson.

But after 1740, with Latin waning, usage of the word *jurisprudence* rose steadily to about 1790, as the last figure shows.

The chief jural idea that I wish to accentuate was a distinction between plain, honest dealings and other, fuzzier ethical duties. Plain, honest dealings were voluntary interactions, with no messing of other people's stuff. If you made money from honest dealings, the result was earnings.

Jurisprudence schooled Europe in a social grammar

Nowadays, an unspecified dirty word is called an expletive, but originally "expletive" meant an unspecified word in a grammatical construction. That might be why Grotius called the grammar-like sense of justice *expletive justice*. It connoted grammar, in particular the relationship between parts of the sentence. Adam Smith and others called it commutative justice. That too connotes part-to-part, just as a commuter travels point-to-point. Part-to-part stands in contradistinction to whole-to-part or part-to-whole.

"The most sacred laws" of commutative justice, Smith said, guard your neighbor's person, property, and promises-due. The rules of its precept are "precise and accurate," or grammar-like (TMS 175.11; 327.1). The precept of commutative justice provides a social grammar.

I say 'precept' to abstract away from what happens once the precept is violated; jurisprudence thusly distinguished between a law's *precept* and its *sanction*. Once messing starts, things of course remain somewhat messy, no matter how thoroughly the law tries to specify sanctions by details of the case. It is the precept, not the sanctions, that Smith touts as "precise and accurate."

The rules of the precept evolved with society, and evolved to be precise and accurate. They were not invented by jural theorists, just as grammar was not invented by grammarians. Sometimes rules remain tacit until theorists study them. Smith said that often the precept of a rule prescribes "no more than common sense dictates to any man tho' he had never heard there was such a rule" (LRBL 73). The time-and-place rules of commutative justice are a prime example of natural convention.

But jural theory did have consequences. The analysis and articulation of customary rules of commutative justice by men like Grotius clarified what counts as honest dealings, for example by analyzing the nature of consent and contract in various circumstances. It considered the sources of ownership. During the Thirty Years War, objects came into people's possession in odd ways: Were they legitimately owned by the current possessor? And what about reputation? Is it covered by commutative justice? Jural theory formulated and clarified what it meant to mess with your neighbor's stuff. It thereby instructed one on what *not* to do.

For equal-equal jural relationships, the drift was, to use the analogy of rules for writing: Write whatever sentences your imagination conjures, but do not violate grammar. With commutative justice pinned down in a time and place, this message was often accompanied by tactful counsel for the jural superior, that is, the rulers or governors: Maybe you should try to abstain from actions which if they were done by an equal in equal-equal relationships would be regarded as criminal. Thus, jurisprudence gave wings to policy precepts that would, beginning in the 1770s, come to be called "liberal."

Jurisprudence kindled focalism and innovism

Let us return to McCloskey's narrative about economic activity. The clarification of commutative justice opened up the hyperspace of having a go—an honest go. Again, not all of it was ethical or virtuous—just as one may write a vicious yet grammatically correct sentence. But a certain presumption was given to honest income, while reservations and exceptions would be matters for the two looser conceptions of justice.

It broke 'having a go' wide open. It wasn't just the traditional vocations of carving stone or baking bread. It was *anything you could imagine*. Thus, two things were happening simultaneous: (1) jural theorists were clarifying the category of honest income, and (2) moral leaders were authorizing the pursuit of honest income.

Honest income is but a part of the individual's local interests. Being more concrete, local interests make for focal points in everyday life. They are matters we can advance effectively, because they are matters of which we have some knowledge and influence. The moral authorization given to focal interests is what Erik Matson (2023) calls *focalism* in an article in the *Journal of the History of Economic Thought*. Focalism is the moral endorsement of focusing on one's local good, within moral constraints, beginning with those clarified by jural theory. Within such moral constraints, focalist efforts generally conduce to the good of the whole. Here we have the spontaneous order meaning of "invisible hand."

The moral authorization of focalism and the conceptual openness of honest income invigorated enterprise like never before. Enterprise and honest innovation became God's work. McCloskey (2016) calls the surge *innovism*: "the frenetic bettering of machines and procedures and institutions after 1800, supported by a startling change in the ethical evaluation of the betterings" (p. 93). Adam Smith quietly called for innovation and dynamism in calling for reform "where every man was *perfectly free* both to chuse what occupation he thought proper, and *to change it as often as he thought proper*" (116, italics added).

The children of jurisprudence are liberalism and liberal political economy

Smith's younger associate Dugald Stewart (1854) wrote that systems of natural jurisprudence provided "the first rudiments...of liberal politics taught in modern times" (26, cf 183). We needed jurisprudence to clarify the abstract category of honest dealings or earnings, which would then be morally authorized, and then be advanced in policy reform, all leading to innovism. We needed jurisprudence to clarify liberty—the government not messing with one's stuff. J.G.A. Pocock (1983) says it succinctly: "the child of jurisprudence is liberalism" (p. 249).

Stewart wrote that it is also to jurisprudence that "we are chiefly indebted for the modern science of Political Economy" (1854, 171). The very concepts of 'the free market' and 'intervention' are rooted in the formulations of commutative justice: not messing with other people's stuff. Jurisprudence was critical to the development of economic thought. The figure below indicates a sharp rise in economic discourse in the 1740s and 1750s.

Liberal heart and liberal spine

Deirdre McCloskey rightly tells us that ideas matter, talk matters, culture matters, moral authorization matters, moral leadership matters. That is how the world works. The evidence of ngrams bolsters her theory.

But what is the good? McCloskey's answer is liberal civilization. A leader for our time, she tells us to cherish it and to identify with it.

The role of jural theory, both historically and conceptually, in the making of the Great Enrichment, though once better understood, fell into neglect. Perhaps it did so because it presents paradoxes and it embarrasses slogans, denials, and taboos. Whatever the reasons for

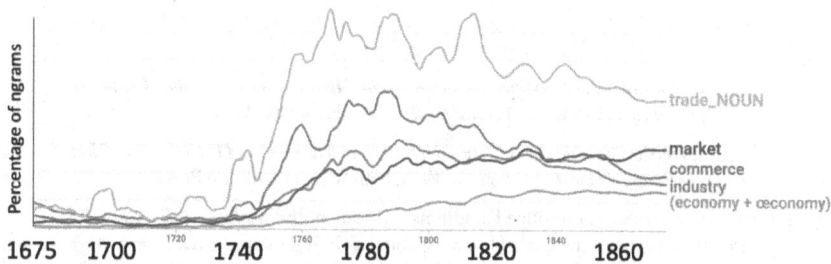

its neglect, the jural theory of Grotius and others clarified and still clarifies the liberty that is at the center of what Smith called "the liberal plan." Benjamin Constant would associate it with 'modern liberty' and Isaiah Berlin with 'negative liberty.' The liberty maxim is the spine of liberal civilization, and we must grapple amicably with the difficulties if we are to maintain and strengthen that spine.

The spine depends on heart. Our future turns on love. The grave menace is the governmentalization of social affairs. We must stand up to ideas and activities which tend toward that evil. The health of the spine begins in the chest.

References

Hallam, Henry. 1839. *Introduction to the Literature of Europe in the Fifteenth, Sixteenth and Seventeenth Centuries.* Harper & Brothers, Publishers.

Hume, David. 1983. *The History of England from the Invasion of Julius Caesar to the Revolution in 1688*, edited by W.B. Todd. 6 vols. Liberty Fund.

Matson, Erik W. 2023. The Edifying Discourses of Adam Smith: Focalism, Commerce, and Serving the Common Good. *Journal of the History of Economic Thought* 45(2): 507–524.

McCloskey, Deirdre N. 2006. *The Bourgeois Virtues: Ethics for an Age of Commerce.* The University of Chicago Press.

McCloskey, Deirdre N. 2010. *Bourgeois Dignity: Why Economics Can't Explain the Modern World*. University of Chicago Press.

McCloskey, Deirdre N. 2016. *Bourgeois Equality: How Ideas, Not Capital or Institutions, Enriched the World*. University of Chicago Press.

McCloskey, Deirdre N. 2019. *Why Liberalism Works: How True Liberal Values Produce a Freer, More Equal, Prosperous World for All*. Yale University Press.

McCloskey, Deirdre N., and Art Carden. 2020. *Leave Me Alone and I'll Make You Rich: How the Bourgeois Deal Enriched the World*. University of Chicago Press.

Pocock, J. G. A. 1983. Cambridge Paradigms and Scotch Philosophers: A Study of the Relations between the Civic Humanist and the Civil Jurisprudential Interpretation of Eighteenth-Century Social Thought. In *Wealth and Virtue: The Shaping of Political Economy in the Scottish Enlightenment*, edited by I. Hont and M. Ignatieff, 235–252. Cambridge University Press.

Stewart, Dugald. 1854. *The Collected Works of Dugald Stewart*, vol. 1: *The Progress of Metaphysical, Ethical, and Political Philosophy since the Revival of Letters in Europe*, ed. W. Hamilton. Constable and Co.

Tierney, Brian. 1997. *The Idea of Natural Rights*. Atlanta: Scholars Press.

Tierney, Brian. 2014. *Liberty & Law: The Idea of Permissive Natural Law, 1100–1800*. Washington, D.C.: Catholic University of America Press.

Tocqueville, Alexis de. 2000. *Democracy in America*. Trans. and ed. by H.C. Mansfield and D. Winthrop. University of Chicago Press.

CHAPTER 4

Adam Smith's Synergistic Moral Authorizations

Erik W. Matson

Commerce, David Hume told us, decays not just where it is insecure, but where it is not honorable (Hume 1994, 93). McCloskey elaborates across her Bourgeois Trilogy how the Great Enrichment came from changing attitudes about work, profit-seeking, and enterprise (McCloskey 2006; 2011; 2016). The Great Enrichment came on the wings of a moral affirmation of the pursuit of honest income.

Clarifying that moral affirmation was the tradition of natural jurisprudence, associated with figures like Francisco Suárez, Hugo Grotius, Samuel von Pufendorf, Richard Cumberland, and Jean Barbeyrac. In the previous chapter, Dan Klein discussed jurisprudence and McCloskey's Great Enrichment. In developing a secular, social grammar, these jural theorists, Klein writes, "were clarifying the category of honest income" just as "moral leaders were authorizing" its pursuit. The synergy between that clarification and authorization bore much fruit.

Klein and McCloskey both point to Smith as a high point in the articulation of bourgeois virtue and the moral affirmation of enterprise. As I've written elsewhere, what Smith called "the liberal plan" in political economy is "liberal" (generous, munificent, giving width to facts and interpretation) in the wide and diverse array of human activities it legitimates (Matson 2022b). Each pursues her interest her own way; she may do so with confidence and presumptive self-appro-bation, so long as she stays within the bounds of justice.

In this essay I unfold Smith's moral authorizations of enterprise and the pursuit of honest income. The authorizations involve virtuous feedback loops between his ethics in *The Theory of Moral Sentiments* and his political economy in *The Wealth of Nations*.

A key ethical principle in TMS is something I call "focalism" in a recent article in the *Journal of the History of Economic Thought* (Matson 2023b). Focalism is about how our attention ought to be directed. In the article I say that focalism maintains that "we ought to princi-pally attend to the objects of our sympathetic affections, beginning with our own person, and then circling outwards, with concurrent-ly diminishing moral obligation, to our family, friends, neighbors, workmates, fellow citizens, and fellow humans anywhere or anytime in the future."

Focalism rests upon three propositions, each supported through-out Smiths' work.

1. **"Ought" implies "can."** We have no obligation to attempt that which is not in our power. If we were to discover people on Mars, we would wish them well, but would have no concrete obligations towards them since they exist entirely beyond our reach (TMS 140.9).

2. **"Can" implies knowledge.** We can't act effectively if we lack local, circumstantial knowledge. To help oth-ers requires us to gather contextual details about their situation, anticipate the probable effects of our aid,

and so forth. The point looms large in Smith's politics (WN 456.10; WN 687.51).

3. **Knowledge is limited by social experience.** We learn about others by engaging with them and sympathizing with them. We are less well-equipped to help those we don't know than those we do. In our relationships we develop relational knowledge, including mutual expectations about moral duties to one another. Relational knowledge begins with our relationship with ourself. We have an immediate obligation to tend to our own needs because we have better knowledge of our hunger, thirst, and so on. Our obligations diminish, on the whole, as familiarity diminishes. Smith captures the point when he says that "the great society of mankind would be best promoted by directing the principal attention of each individual to that particular portion of it, which was most within the sphere of both his abilities and of his understanding" (TMS 229.4).

In our efforts to serve the good, focalism teaches us to orient our efforts around a "humbler department" than the abstract care of humankind in general: "the care of [our] own happiness, of that of [our] family, [our] friends, [our] country" (TMS 237.6). F.A. Hayek communicates the idea this way: "all man's mind can effectively comprehend are the facts of the narrow circle of which he is the centre" (Hayek 2012, 59).

The focalism in TMS is complemented by key insights of WN. Those insights illustrate how tending to our "humbler departments" in fact serves the common good of humankind. As we focus on concrete duties of care for self, family, and community, we may, so long as our acts stay within the bounds of commutative justice, be said to serve the good of humankind generally, in part because self, family, and community form parts of the whole of humankind. Smith shows us that as we bring our goods and services to the marketplace, as we innovate and strive to better our condition, we unwittingly participate in a grand, global concatenation. That concatenation is metaphorically coordinated by the price system, which in turn relies on shared conventions of ownership and contract.

Virtuous feedback loops

As indicated in Figure 1, focalism and liberal political economy are bidirectionally reinforcing.

FIGURE 1

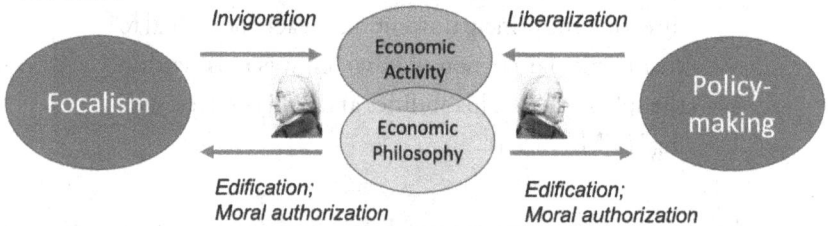

Reflections on the limits of our knowledge lead us towards the principle of focalism. As we understand the limits of our power and influence, we rightly feel that it is proper for us to focus on that which we can influence—our personal well-being and the well-being of our familiars. As we reflect on the teachings of liberal political economy, we come to see how a focus on these humbler departments serves the good of the many. Smith helps us see that the pursuit of honest income might be a species of what James Buchanan called "benevolent self-interest" (in Buchanan and Yoon 1994, 340). The pursuit of honest income channels our interests to serve the good of the whole. We can think of the pursuit of honest income as either a literal or metaphorical cooperation with God in serving the good of humankind. That notion inheres in Smith's "invisible hand."

The relation between focalism and liberal political economy may be said to influence Smith's teachings on policymaking throughout WN. With a sense of the propriety of private enterprise and its benefits, Smith advances a presumption of liberty in public policy, whereby violations of liberty (understood essentially as the negative freedom that comes with each person's bodily sovereignty and ownership of property) bear the burden of proof. Smith's liberalism does not derive deductively or axiomatically from first principles, but, like the sensibilities of his teacher Francis Hutcheson, stems from a conviction that freedom best serves the common good (see Matson 2023a).

By removing barriers to market entry, lifting trade restrictions, diminishing government subsidies, repealing government-granted monopoly privilege, and allowing for labor mobility, liberalization in public policy frees economic activity. Freedom extends and complexifies the division of labor, reinforcing the logic of focalism—as the world become more complex, our knowledge of things beyond our narrow circle of familiarity further diminishes. Reinforcing the logic of focalism spreads the general sense of the propriety of "having a go," so to speak, among the population, further inspiriting the economy. As this inspiriting runs its course it displays the truths of the teachings of liberal economic theory—new forms of organization in industry, innovations and capital accumulation, further subdivision in production all serve to increase the quality and quantity of output, all the while providing individuals with greater scope of opportunity. In turn, such developments further authorize liberalization in policy.

In Figure 1, the images of Smith represent aspects of his efforts in moral education across his works. He looked to inform citizens of modern, commercial polities of their duties and obligations towards one another. He was a part of building what J.G.A. Pocock has called a "commercial humanism" (1985, 50). He looked to teach his readers that honest industry and attention to our focal relations is, especially in the complex realties of the modern world, perhaps the most effective way that most of us can serve the good of humankind.

Let's look at each of the four arrows in Figure 1, beginning in the top left part of the picture: the arrow from focalism to economic activity.

Focalism and Economic Invigoration

Smith tells us in WN that each person naturally desires to better his or her condition, but not how each understands betterment. In TMS we learn of the strong desire each of us has for praise and approval from our fellows. What our fellows approve of partially conditions how we understand circumstantial improvement.

For much of human history, commercial enterprise was understood as a necessary but somewhat degrading activity. Merchants, traders, and craftsmen were viewed with suspicion. As of the late Middle Ages, honor and praise were conferred on those privileged with political and religious authority. In the Western Christian tradition, right and holy living was often understood in terms of contemplation and removal from the temptations and distractions of mundane life. These sensibilities depressed commercial spirit, even where the requisite institutions for an extended commerce largely obtained, as in England.

Out of the Renaissance, attitudes about the dignity of commerce and, more generally, the character of virtue began to change. Northern Christian humanist discourse (particularly the writings of Erasmus) and then Protestant theology emphasized the virtues of social engagement and activity over cloistered living. Martin Luther taught that although God does not need our good works (they are irrelevant for our salvation), our neighbors do (see Wingren 1957). In faith we look upwards to God. Transformed by faith, in love we look outwards to our neighbor. Through our ordinary work, we cooperate with God in bringing his kindness and provision to others.

In the seventeenth century, thanks in part to jural theorizing, notions of honest trade entered public discourse. Trade and commerce came to be understood as callings (God-appointed tasks), for example in the teachings of prominent Puritan divines like William Perkins and Richard Baxter. Changing conceptions of commerce, at least in England, come across in the title of Richard Steele's (1629-1692) enormously popular *The Tradesman's Calling*, in which he argued that "every Pin and Nail in the Building, how obscure soever, concurs to the Beauty and Strength of the [whole] Work" (Steele 1684, 28).

Smith's discourse belongs to this flow of changing sensibilities about commercial enterprise. In the first chapter of WN he tells how even a "course and rough" woolen coat of the "day-labourer" is the "produce of the joint labour of a great multitude" (WN 22.11). There is beauty beneath the surface even in so mundane a good. Being sensible to that beauty morally authorizes participants to continue in their humble tasks with focus and diligence, even verve and alacrity. That authorization invigorates economic activity by depicting humble commercial tasks as laudable, even sanctified.

The ethic of focalism teaches the limitations of disinterested benevolence. Because the knowledge required to serve the good is, in most cases, developed circumstantially, we are unable to effectively serve the good outside of our relational networks. If we would serve what a universally benevolent spectator would approve of, then, we should diligently focus on our humbler departments. In a free political and economic order, that focus brings us to cooperate with others, each of whom is focusing on his or her humbler departments; together we serve the good of the whole by tending to our parts. In these activities, we may not be able to tout our own benevolence or beneficence, but we can claim *beneficialness*.

Economic philosophy and focalism

Ideas about focalism were developed from Stoic ideas prior to Smith by Shaftesbury, Hutcheson and especially Joseph Butler (Matson 2022a). Those ideas complemented the burgeoning theological discourse on work and calling. In the eighteenth century, economics provided new analytical justification for the notion of commerce as a divine calling. Smith's analysis of the division of labor, the "higgling and bargaining" of the price system (WN I.v.4), and the coordinating function of speculation, and much more, elucidate how our humble efforts serve the good.

Smith's economic philosophy teaches us about the correspondence—or lack thereof—between the interest of each part and that of the whole. In grain markets, for example, it is the grain speculator or "the inland dealer" and not the prudent statesman who most effectively wards off famine: "the interest of the inland dealer, and that of the great body of the people, how opposite soever they may at first appear, are, even in years of greatest scarcity, exactly the same" (WN 524.3).

In this lesson, along with many others throughout WN, Smith is not condoning the neglect of our fellows. Rather, in illustrating the workings of the economy he casts light on how working to better our condition and the condition of our familiars serves the good of strangers—more effectively, on the whole, than through ad hoc policy intervention.

Economic philosophy reinforces the ethic of focalism by spelling out in greater analytic detail how "God" cares for "the universal happiness of all rational and sensible beings" (TMS 237.6), as it were, through our ordinary pursuits.

Economic philosophy and policymaking

Now we turn to the arrows on the righthand side of Figure 1. Smith's economic philosophy culminates in "the liberal plan of equality, liberty, and justice" under which each person can pursue "his own interest his own way" (WN 664.51). The liberal plan cites economic analysis in its own justification; but we shouldn't neglect its ethical provenance in ideas about the dignity of work. Our labor is "sacred and inviolable" (WN 138.12).

In WN Smith focuses on bringing about four main kinds of reforms: free choice in occupation, free trade in land, free domestic trade, and free international commerce (Viner 1927). But he applies his liberal sensibilities to other areas of policy as well: "Let the same natural liberty of exercising what species of industry they please be restored to all his majesty's subjects" (WN 470.42).

WN advances a presumption of liberty in policymaking. Smith understands, according to Charles Griswold, that

> the state may intervene in all sorts of ways, but those who would have it do so are required to show why it should in this particular instance, for how long, in precisely what fashion, and how its intervention will escape the usual dangers of creating entrenched interest groups and self-perpetuating monopolies. (Griswold 1999, 295)

Policymaking and economic activity: Completing the loop

In conjunction with changing cultural attitudes about commerce, liberalization frees and encourages economic activity. Smith sought to repeal the laws of settlement and statues of apprenticeship—initially enacted under Elizabeth I as the Statute of Artificers in 1562—to enable workers, by allowing them greater freedom, to develop skills and bring their labor to market. He worked towards freer domestic and international trade to extend the division of labor, encourage specialization, and increase technical progress, which would raise living standards and create new opportunities and new markets for refined goods and services.

Moral authorizations of, on the one hand, honest income and, on the other, of policy liberalization spelled the Great Enrichment, the fruit of which billions of people now enjoy. One of the patron saints of the Great Enrichment, Smith teaches how we do our part in serving the good of the whole; how in focusing diligently on the good of our part we serve that of the whole; and how freedom fortifies the remarkable correspondence between those two goods.

References

Buchanan, James M., and Yong J. Yoon, eds. 1994. *The Return to Increasing Returns. Anne Arbor: University of Michigan Press.*

Griswold, Charles L. 1999. *Adam Smith and the Virtues of Enlightenment.* New York: Cambridge University Press.

Hayek, F.A. 2012. *Studies on the Abuse and Decline of Reason: Text and Documents.* Edited by Bruce Caldwell. London and New York: Routledge.

Hume, David. 1994. *Essays, Moral, Political, and Literary.* Edited by Eugene F. Miller. Indianapolis: Liberty Fund.

Matson, Erik W. 2022a. "Butler and Smith's Ethical and Theological Framing of Commerce." In *Adam Smith, Theology, and Morality,* edited by J. Ballor and C. van der

Kooi, 189–213. London: Routledge.

Matson, Erik W. 2022b. "What Is Liberal about Adam Smith's 'Liberal Plan'?" *Southern Economic Journal* 89 (2): 593–610.

Matson, Erik W. 2023a. "Commerce as Cooperation with the Deity: Self-Love, the Common Good, and the Coherence of Francis Hutcheson." *The European Journal of the History of Economic Thought* 30 (4): 507–24.

Matson, Erik W. 2023b. "The Edifying Discourse of Adam Smith: Focalism, Commerce, and Serving the Common Good." *Journal of the History of Economic Thought* 46 (2): 298–320. https://doi.org/10.1017/S1053837221000353.

McCloskey, Deirdre N. 2006. *The Bourgeois Virtues: Ethics for an Age of Commerce.* Chicago: The University of Chicago Press.

McCloskey, Deirdre N. 2011. *Bourgeois Dignity: Why Economics Can't Explain the Modern World. Paperback.* Chicago and London: University of Chicago Press.

McCloskey, Deirdre N. 2016. *Bourgeois Equality: How Ideas, Not Capital or Institutions, Enriched the World.* Chicago and London: University of Chicago Press.

Pocock, J.G.A. 1985. "Clergy and Commerce: The Conservative Enlightenment in England." In *L'Eta Dei Lumi: Studi Storici Sul Settecento Europeo in Onore Di Franco Venturi,* 1:525–62. Naples: Jovene.

Steele, Richard. 1684. *The Tradesman's Calling. Being a Discourse Concerning the Nature, Necessity, Choice &c. of a Calling in General: And Directions for the Right Managing of the Tradesman's Calling in Particular.* London: Samuel Sprint.

Viner, Jacob. 1927. "Adam Smith and Laissez Faire." *Journal of Political Economy* 35 (2): 198–232.

Wingren, Gustaf. 1957. *Luther on Vocation.* Translated by Carl C. Rasmussen. Oregon: Wipf & Stock.

CHAPTER 5

David Hume on the Common Law and English Liberty

Jacob R. Hall

I n a 2022 *Political Theory* article, Paul Sagar treats Adam Smith, David Hume, and Montesquieu on the origins and robustness of English liberty. Sagar says that "Smith took more seriously than Hume the idea that liberty required not just an appropriate constitution but quotidian security as realized via law" (2022, 398). Sagar goes further to say that Hume would underestimate, or miss entirely, the idea "that liberty must be understood not just in terms of the form of constitution and wider political order, but also regarding the security of citizens as achieved via the legal system, and especially the operation of fair trials" (ibid., 394).

When getting down to the historical specifics, Sagar charges Hume with overlooking the importance of the common law for English liberty. He says that Smith, in contrast to Hume, considered the common law, and particular the legal reforms of Edward I (r. 1272-1307), as a major component in the story of English liberty.

I do not dispute Sagar's reading of Smith. The common law was an important element of English liberty, and Smith understood that well.

But so did Hume. In response to Sagar, I published a comment in *Econ Journal Watch* (Hall 2022). What follows here is the core of Hume's narrative of the emergence and significance of the common law. Here I quote from Volumes 1 and 2 of Hume's *The History of England* eight times, and cite them 32 times in all. Yet more from those two volumes is used in Hall (2022). These citations show that Hume did not lack what Sagar suggests he lacked. Sagar himself never once quotes or cites Volume 1 and 2 of Hume's *History*. Sagar's article tends to drive a wedge between two thinkers who, rather, thought very much along the same lines on the history and institutional groundings of law and liberty, with Smith promoting and developing the thought of Hume.

Jural integration and law in medieval England

From King Arthur to Henry VIII, England was ruled by multiple, competing powers. In volumes 1 and 2 of the *History*, Hume shows us, often in bloody detail, the fragility of the authority and legitimacy of the average medieval king (H, 2:283–284). In addition to the king, England was home to a number of powerful actors, such as the towns, independent barons, and the Roman Catholic Church and its affiliate ecclesiastical bodies, not to mention the potential influence of the Welsh, Scottish, and French aristocracies. Each separate authority had its own jurisdiction, source of power and influence, and instruments for making its voice heard.

The existence of multiple powers capable of violence made medieval England a dangerous place to live. "Every profession was held in contempt but that of arms" (*H*, 1:463). Every medieval king, no matter how secure on his throne, at some point found himself face to face with either a rival claimant or a cabal of aggrieved barons. The barons, moreover, routinely engaged in private warfare, leaving the countryside in a continual state of chaos and lawlessness (*H*, 1:231, 237, 250, 284, 288, 350–351, 371–372, 400, 463, 2:11, 143, 189, 279). Even during periods of relative peace, "men were never secure in their houses" and bands of robbers, often supported by encastellated barons, were known to plunder entire villages (*H*, 1:69, 288). Hume characterizes medieval England as an environment of political instability and low growth (*H*, 1:463).

A main theme of Hume's *History* is the integration of the separate powers into a single unified government (Forbes 1975, 263; Whelan 2004, 256; Sabl 2012, 65). Dan Klein and I have produced a lengthy compendium that gives 142 quotations from Hume's *History* touching upon jural pluralism or jural integration (Hall and Klein 2020). Barry Weingast (2015; 2016; 2017) identifies similar themes in Smith's *Wealth of Nations* and *Lectures on Jurisprudence*. Integration went hand-in-hand with the increasing power and authority of the king. It was a slow process—two steps forward, one step back. The personal characters of kings were of great importance, as evidenced by both Hume's historical narrative and his lengthy character portraits.

Up to the Tudors, the strongest and most respectable of kings seemed to sire the weakest and least respectable heirs. Henry II begets John, and Edward I begets Edward II.

Still, through the centuries, the authority of the king increased in scale and in scope. Individual kings may have been weak, but the crown grew stronger. The medieval era eventually gave way to what we now call the early modern period. We might say that medieval gave way to early modern at the Battle of Bosworth Field in 1485 when Henry Tudor won the War of the Roses, crushing Richard III and his supporters in the process. Henry VII (r. 1485-1509) and Henry VIII (r. 1509-1547) crafted reforms that eventually demilitarized the English aristocracy (H, 3:75, 77). By the time Hume discusses the reign of Elizabeth I (r. 1558-1603) in Volume 4, the competing powers of the medieval era have fallen away and he speaks of the government.

At the height of the medieval era, the rules enforced in the King's court were in semi-competition with the other courts of the realm. An aggrieved man could seek justice in the county courts which administered local customary law or he could go to the ecclesiastical courts which administered canon law. A town merchant could take his case to a borough court to be judged by the rules of the *Lex mercatoria*. One might even go to one's feudal lord to make his case under the rules of feudal custom. The royal law, however, was common throughout the realm and was the origination point of what has come to be known as the common law (Hogue 1986).

Arthur Hogue (1986) defined common law as "the body of rules prescribing social conduct and justiciable in the royal courts of England" (5), and I use the phrase common law along those lines. At a more abstract level, common law is simply law held in common throughout the polity. Yet another sense of common law is law worked out through precedent. All of these senses of common law are rooted in the historical development of English common law. The royal law applied to all Englishmen, no matter where the crime was committed or who the perpetrator may have been. As royal judges travelled the kingdom hearing cases, they learned and refined their legal judgments. By travelling, they made the royal law common throughout the realm. Through their travels they amassed a bank of precedent that they could call upon in subsequent cases.

Over time, the common law, enforced by the royal courts, subsumed or marginalized its competitors. As the authority and power of the king grew the "justice done in the king's name by men who [were] the king's servants became the most important kind of justice" (Pollock and Maitland 1895, 91). The success of the common law went hand in hand with the centralization of power around the king. Hume said as much:

> It [the people's freedom] required the authority almost
> absolute of the sovereigns, which took place in the subse-

quent period, to pull down those disorderly and licentious tyrants, who were equally averse from peace and from freedom, and to establish that regular execution of the laws which, in a following age, enabled the people to erect a regular and equitable plan of liberty. (*H*, 2:525)

As the king's power and authority grew, so did the impact of his laws. Frederick Pollock and Frederic Maitland (1895), Arthur Hogue (1966), Harold Berman (1983), and John Baker (1995), all scholars of the common law, attest to that fact.

Another reason for the rise of the common law cited by Hume was the rediscovery of Justinian's Pandects, a compendium of juristic writings on Roman law. For Hume, the rediscovery in 1130 of Justinian's Pandects was a glimmer of light from a more civilized era that would begin to illuminate a dark world. No other event "tended further to the improvement of the age" (*H*, 2:520).

With Justinian's Pandects in their hands, the clergy took up legal studies with great zeal. Less than ten years later, according to Hume, lectures in civil law were being given in Oxford. Although Roman civil law never rose to the same level of prominence in England as it did on the continent (and in Scotland) it nonetheless left a permanent mark on English law (*H*, 2:520–521). The English jurists imitated their civil law equivalents, "rais[ing] their own law from its original state of rudeness and imperfection" (*H*, 2:521). Here Hume complements Larry Siedentop's *Inventing the Individual* (2014) on the importance of Christianity and the Catholic Church for the development of western liberalism.

Hume's treatment of the common law

To find Hume's discussions of concrete legal developments, we need to look at his coverage of the strongest medieval English kings: Henry II and Edward I—the same kings recognized by Adam Smith in his narration of the common law in his Lectures, as highlighted by Paul Sagar. Of the medieval English kings, only Henry II and Edward I were able to extend their authority and carry out reform without having their political coalitions turn on them.

The reign of King Stephen (r. 1135–1154) was marked by "The Anarchy"—a succession crisis that led to the complete breakdown of civil order in England (*H*, 1:279–295). Henry II (r. 1154–1189), upon winning the war and ascending to the throne, was tasked with cleaning up the mess and restoring order and justice to the kingdom. Hume depicts Henry II as a good and strong king who led England with a steady hand and an "equitable administration" (*H*, 1:359, 301, 370). He was a politically savvy man, as shown by his swift actions to demolish the castles illegally built by the local barons during "The Anarchy" (*H*, 1:360). He had his share of dark days (*H*, 1:310–338, 348–358), as all medieval kings did, but he was responsible for increasing the power of the monarchy over the licentious barons and executing long-lasting reforms to England's legal system.

In 1176, Henry II partitioned England into four divisions and appointed itinerant justices to travel along a circuit to hear and decide on the cases brought before them in the counties (*H*, 1:359–360). The general "eyre," as the law circuit was called, extended the geographic reach of the king's court and furthered the mission of making the king's law common throughout the realm. The eyre increased the geographical influence of the king's laws and accustomed Englishmen to its regular enforcement. It protected the lower gentry and the peasants from the arbitrary violence and corruption of the barons, and, albeit slowly, acted to curb baronial power (*H*, 1:360). Hume illustrates how Henry II's actions furthered England down the road toward an integrated nation-state.

The coercive power of the monarchy goes a long way. But the expansion of royal justice and the common law was not a matter of mere force. Royal justice passed the market test and came to be the preferred court of law because it administered better justice. The eyre justices were seen as men of honor, in contrast to the local courts, thus the respectability of the common law was bolstered by their character (*H*, 1:360). They were better trained and less corrupt than their local counterparts.

After looking at the common law reforms under Henry II, Hume drops common law until his discussion of Edward I (r. 1272–1307). That is understandable. What occupies Hume during the reigns of Richard I (r. 1189–1199), John (r. 1199–1215), and Henry III (r. 1216–1272) are the events leading to John's capitulation at Runnymede and the solidification of Magna Carta into the English political ethos. Like Henry II, Edward I inherited a mess. Edward's father, Henry III, was a relatively weak king who bumbled his way into a civil war with a group of barons led by Simon de Montfort. Upon inheriting the crown, Edward "immediately applied himself to the re-establishment of his kingdom, and to the correcting of those disorders" introduced by Henry III's weak administration (*H*, 2:75).

Edward I was a strong king. As recognized by Smith and discussed by Sagar, Edward I was a great legal and constitutional reformer. Smith puts Edward I alongside Henry II as one of the greats in terms of his legislative capacity (*LJ*(A), v.34).

Hume's account of Edward I's legal reforms is similar to Smith's. To diminish the power of the great barons, Edward offered his protection to the gentry, merchants, and serfs by instituting "an exact distribution of justice" and by "a rigid execution of the laws" (*H*, 2:75). He did so by insisting that as he obeyed Magna Carta with respect to the barons, they too should extend and uphold Magna Carta with respect to their own vassals. He replaced corrupt judges and provided the justice system as a whole with force sufficient to execute the law properly (*H*, 2:75). Hume says that by Edward's actions "the face of the kingdom was soon changed; and order and justice took place of violence and oppression" (*H*, 2:75–76). In fact, Hume argues that Edward's legal reforms were the chief advantage which the English attained from his reign—and even more importantly, that Englishmen "still continue to reap" the benefits of Edward's vigor in Hume's day (*H*, 2:141).

Hume's narrative of the common law is similar to Smith's. The style of Hume's *History* and Smith's LJ differ, or course. Smith lectured to students whereas Hume wrote for mass consumption. But their estimation of the importance of the common law for the development of English liberty is equal. Smith understood "that liberty required not just an appropriate constitution but quotidian security as realized via law" (Sagar 2022, 398). So did Hume.

References

Baker, John H. 1995. Personal Liberty Under the Common Law of England, 1200–1600. In *The Origins of Modern Freedom in the West*, ed. R. W. Davis, 178–202. Stanford, Cal.: Stanford University Press.

Berman, Harold J. 1983. *The Formation of the Western Legal Tradition*. Cambridge, Mass.: Harvard University Press.

Forbes, Duncan. 1985. *Hume's Philosophical Politics*. London: Cambridge University Press.

Hall, Jacob R. 2022. From Hume to Smith on the Common Law and English Liberty: A Comment on Paul Sagar. *Econ Journal Watch* 19(1): 109-123.

Hall, Jacob R., and Daniel B. Klein. 2020. Jural Pluralism and Jural Integration in David Hume's History of England: A Compendium of 142 Quotes. GMU Working Paper in Economics 20-36 (George Mason University, Fairfax, Va.).

Hogue, Arthur. 1986 [1966]. *Origins of the Common Law*. Indianapolis: Liberty Fund.

Hume, David. 1983 (H). *The History of England from the Invasion of Julius Caesar to the Revolution in 1688*, ed. W. B. Todd, 6 vols. Indianapolis: Liberty Fund.

Hume, David. 1994. *Essays, Moral, Political, and Literary*, ed. Eugene F. Miller. Indianapolis: Liberty Fund.

Klein, Daniel B., and Erik W. Matson. 2020. Mere-Liberty in David Hume. In *A Companion to David Hume*, ed. Moris Polanco, 125–160. Guatemala City: Universidad Francisco Marroquin.

Pollock, Frederick, and Frederic Maitland. 2010 [1895]. *The History of English Law before the Time of Edward I*, 2 vols. Indianapolis: Liberty Fund.

Sabl, Andrew. 2012. *Hume's Politics*. Princeton, N.J.: Princeton University Press.

Sagar, Paul. 2022. On the Liberty of the English: Adam Smith's Reply to Montesquieu and Hume. *Political Theory 50(3): 381–404.*

Smith, Adam. 1976 [1776] (WN). *The Wealth of Nations*, ed. R. H. Campbell and A. S. Skinner, 2 vols. Oxford, UK: Oxford University Press.

Smith, Adam. 1982 (LJ). *Lectures on Jurisprudence*, ed. R. L. Meek, D. D. Raphael, and P. G. Stein. Oxford, UK: Oxford University Press.

Weingast, Barry R. 2015. Adam Smith's Industrial Organization of Religion: Explaining the Medieval Church's Monopoly and Its Breakdown in the Reformation. Working paper.

Weingast, Barry R. 2016. The Medieval Expansion of Long-Distance Trade: Adam Smith on the Town's Escape from the Violent and Low-Growth Feudal Equilibrium. Stanford Law and Economics Olin Working Paper 492 (Stanford University, Stanford, Cal.).

Weingast, Barry R. 2017. Adam Smith's Theory of Violence and the Political Economics of Development. In *Organizations, Civil Society, and the Roots of Development*, ed. Naomi R. Lamoreaux and John Joseph Wallis, 51–82. Chicago: University of Chicago Press.

Whelan, Frederick G. 2004. *Hume and Machiavelli: Political Realism and Liberal Thought.* Lanham, Md.: Lexington Books.

CHAPTER 6

William James' Pragmatism and Adam Smith's Moral Sentiments

Marcus Shera

Those who maintain the notion of an is-ought gap often appeal to a passage in David Hume's *A Treatise of Human Nature*. It should be remembered that Hume disavowed the *Treatise* and that the suggestion of an is-ought gap does not arise in any of his subsequent writings (Klein 2017). Moreover, interpretations of the original passage vary.[1]

The embrace of an is-ought gap sometimes goes with readings of Adam Smith's *The Theory of Moral Sentiments* (TMS) as a descriptive work of moral psychology rather than an endeavor in moral education. Smith himself indicates at one point that his inquiry is "a matter of fact" and not "a matter of right" (TMS 77.10). That "matter of fact," however, concerns the principles upon which man approves of the punishment of bad actions. I see Smith in TMS as ranging over moral psychology and ethics. He maintains a two-way bridge between concrete moral problems to matters more intellectual and abstract.

In Part III of TMS, Smith compares the judgments of poets and men of letters to mathematicians and natural philosophers in the same

---

1. For an argument that Hume worked to dissolve the distinction between ises and oughts, see Nicholas Capaldi (1989).

manner that he treats the judgments of a man in the street approving or disapproving of the conduct of his neighbors (124.18-23). Smith is concerned with the notion of propriety in both mathematical discourses and in moral sermons. He even speaks of recognizing a certain degree of laughter as proper in proportion to the funniness of a joke (16.1).

Around the turn of the twentieth century, William James led a school of philosophy, drawing on the writings of his friend Charles Saunders Peirce, called "Pragmatism".[1] James's main idea is that the meaningfulness of a belief always relates to its practical implications. The difference between belief and disbelief in a proposition makes a difference in how one engages with the world. Every sort of thinker for James, from the laborer lending attention to his tools to the philosopher writing a treatise, tacitly relates his or her thought to some practical aspect of life. The belief that an all-knowing and all-powerful God exists has "cash value", as James would say: Believing in such a God, I cannot expect to hide from him; I expect him to have the final say in the narrative of the universe; I must attempt to live according to his standards. If a belief in a proposition does not recommend any changes in my active habits, including my sentimental habits, investigating that proposition cannot be part of truth-seeking. The question of whether God is pink or blue, on its face, would seem to be one such proposition.

The relationship between meaning and practicality underlies James's pragmatist theory of truth. He treated the inner life of the mind as coextensive with the outer life of our bodily conduct. "Truth" refers to ideas thought good, that is, thought worth believing, or put-

---

1. James (1908) called the pragmatist philosophy "A New Name for Some Old Ways of Thinking." He said that Socrates, Aristotle, Locke, Berkeley, and Hume all had made significant contributions to truth by using the pragmatic method, but they did not see it as a philosophy with a universal mission.

ting stock in. James wrote: "[T]ruth is *one species of good*, and not, as is usually supposed, a category distinct from good, and co-ordinate with it" (James 1908, 75). The proposition that some idea is true but not something that one ought to believe would be absurd. That an action is good and that one ought to do it correspond by construction, and the same goes for truth and belief. James proposes that we commit to that way of thinking and speaking. (It is good to do so!) When the action is believing a statement about reality, then, if it is deemed good, we say the statement is 'true.' That is not to say we are always right to do so. People disagree about many things about reality, and they cannot all be right. Meaningful beliefs come with practical habits, and the value of those habits is a test of truth.

A proposition about reality that a woman named Beth deems good is a *belief* of Beth's. It is a *true* belief if Beth does so properly or justly; and in that case it has, James says, a "marriage-function" between Beth and the object of belief. Though the object of belief may exist independent of any knower, we can only say that ideas about that object are true. Truth happens to ideas. Beliefs are fashioned like a set of armor from raw ore and scraps of leather. Armor is not functional until it is crafted, and an idea is not true until it fits the believer's movements or doings in the world. James (1908, 69) writes, "[Pragmatism] converts the absolutely empty notion of a static relation of 'correspondence'... between our minds and reality, into that of a rich and active commerce...between particular thoughts of ours, and the great universe of other experiences in which they play their parts and have their uses." James is saying that the system of correspondence that our mind develops is developed for service to our purposes.

Thinking is complicit in acting, and acting complicit in thinking. The virtuous man must be wise, and the wise man virtuous. Your mental activity is a cardinal faculty that has to be nurtured along with virtues manifested in bodily motions, including writing and speech.

"Truth for us is simply a collective name for verification-processes, just as health, wealth, strength, etc., are names for other processes connected with life, and also pursued because it pays to pursue them. Truth is MADE, just as health, wealth and strength are made" (James 1908, 218).

The pragmatist conception of truth makes apparent the implicit "ought" in every "is". Michael Polanyi argued that every statement that "X is true" involves the tacit claim "I believe X," and likely by extension "you ought to believe it too" (1962, 267). Saying that "X is true" is a practical "ought" statement for how we should relate to some part of the world. Polanyi separates each sentence into the articulate content of the sentence, and the assertion that the sentence is true tacit in its utterance.

"Ises" correspond to "oughts". Furthermore, when we recognize that 'ought' derives from the verb 'to owe,' we see 'ought' statements as statements about what one being owes another being, and thus the 'ought' statement is every bit as much an 'is' statement as "Jim owes Mary ten pounds." The distinctiveness of 'ought' statements is a distinctiveness among fellow 'is' statements; it is not a distinctiveness that makes them something other than 'is' statements. Finally, if the emotivist interprets "You ought to do X" as "You doing X is my desire," he has in that fashion shown how "oughts" correspond to "ises," and if we should care about the speaker's approval or disapproval, then those 'ises' are pertinent.

In his 1902 lectures on religious experience at Edinburgh, James said: "What God hath joined together, let no man put asunder. The Continental schools of philosophy have too often overlooked the fact that man's thinking is organically connected with his conduct. It seems to me to be the chief glory of English and Scottish thinkers to have kept the organic connection in view" (1905, 442-3).

One can build a strong case for that "organic connection" in the

Theory of Moral Sentiments. Daniel Klein (2020) finds an angle by the way that Smith uses the word "justice." Building from Smith's paragraph on senses of the word *justice* (269-270.10), Klein finds three uses of "justice" in TMS. First is "commutative justice," the simple abstention from another's 'stuff' (person, property, and promises-due). Second is "distributive justice," the proper and becoming use of one's own resources. Third is "estimative justice," granting the proper degree of admiration or esteem towards some object and pursuing it accordingly.[1] It is the third sense that primarily concerns us here.

Klein finds 68 instances where Smith uses "just" as estimative justice, 36 of which are from TMS (2020, 94, 98). That beliefs, estimations, and systems of thought are practically relevant objects is not lost on Smith (although a statement at TMS 315.3 is exoterically quite otherwise). Smith treats a mental faculty as an ethical one by treating estimating or judging as an action, a phenomenon stemming from the will (TMS 122.6, 130.32). The title of TMS highlights sentiments, themselves a mental phenomenon, and with a natural relation to the actions they motivate. Discovering the analogy between the act of judging and bodily acts helps us think about a Smithian theory of intellectual propriety. Within estimative justice, we might delineate a province in which the object for estimation is something we call an idea, notion, theory, hypothesis, philosophy, school of thought, and so on, and we might call that province of estimative justice epistemic justice.

For moral sentiments, the object of contemplation in TMS is a person's conduct, including her believing, say, a philosophical system or a theory. Her belief in these objects involves judgments which we may find agreeable or disagreeable. Smith compares the sentiments of mathematicians and poets, saying that mathematicians are less con-

---

1. "Estimative justice" is a term coined by Klein (2021) which Smith speaks of without naming it (270.10).

cerned with public opinion (123-126). The curiosity is how seamlessly Smith compares the truth of a mathematical theorem with the beauty of poetry, two things often considered apples and oranges. The differences he finds between the mathematician and the poet have more to do with the precision, accuracy, or determinateness that the mathematician finds in his theorem without the approval of others. Many writers since Smith's time have spoken of such features as the theorem's 'objectivity,' whereas the disagreement and uncertainty over a poem's beauty is said to arise from its lack of 'objectivity.' Smith understands that poets are seeking something less certain than the objects in the quarry of mathematicians. The level of certainty or 'accuracy' that their object of estimation affords speaks to the way in which humans relate to aspects of the world. But that there is a beauty to be pursued in poetry and a truth in mathematics or physics is never abandoned.

Smith a few times seems to distinguish between "moral" and "intellectual" virtues. For example, "[Superior prudence] necessarily supposes the utmost perfection of all the intellectual and of all the moral virtues" (216.15). When Smith speaks about the sympathy we have with another person as the two of us judge a matter with no particular connection to either of us, he elaborates on the man of attention, taste, and superior justness who leads us into deeper and more wonderful understandings of the same object. The praise we bestow on the intellectual leader is due to his "intellectual virtues" (20.3). The distinction is not so interesting as the fact that 'intellectual virtue' is easily and naturally interpreted as a species of 'moral,' since thinking is a type of acting, like talking, if only to oneself, and thus can be estimated for its propriety or beauty. That way of contemplating the intellect solidifies the organic connection between thinking and conduct that James found in the British tradition.

The Theory of Moral Sentiments offers a set of descriptive statements about human judgments, but those statements often imply further statements about Smith's judgments about what it is good to do, including believe. The pragmatist approach impels us to see Smith's claims as a guide to the human faculties of judgment. In order to improve his readers' ability to judge, Smith teaches us the features of our judging apparatus, and how our apparatus relates to that of others. We judge better when our sense of duty is directed towards a higher impartial spectator—the one to whom 'oughts' are owed. A hidden faith of all who make judgments of any kind is that there are good judgments to make. Reading TMS as but a work of moral psychology takes a silent or agnostic position as to the reality of goodness. Smith maintains the reality of goodness; he presupposes the reality of justice; he sustains a reality commitment—just as his friend Hume teaches us to. As Erik Matson (2018) writes in the *Adam Smith Review*, Smith's 'wonder' and surprise—at himself!—at the end of Smith's "History of Astronomy" is perhaps an ironic way of teaching us that even those most self-consciously pragmatist should be equally conscious of their reality commitment.

A proto-pragmatist reading may help those who read TMS as psychology and not moral philosophy, and it may also bring more attention to Smith as a member of the canon of philosophizing about epistemology.

References

Capaldi, Nicholas. 1989. *Hume's Place in Moral Philosophy*. New York: Peter Lang Publishing.

James, William. 1905. *The Varieties of Religious Experience*. Oxfordshire: Routledge.

James, William. 1908. What Pragmatism Means. In *Pragmatism: A New Name for Some Old Ways of Thinking*. New York: Routledge.

Klein, Daniel B. 2017. Foreward to "Glimpses of David Hume." *Econ Journal Watch* 14(3): 474-487.

Klein, Daniel B. 2020. Commutative, Distributive, and Estimative Justice in Adam Smith. In *The Adam Smith Review: Volume 20, ed.* Fonna Forman, 82-102. London: Routledge.

Matson, Erik W. 2018. Adam Smith's Humean Attitude Towards Science; Illustrated by "The History of Astronomy." In *The Adam Smith Review*: Volume 11, ed. Fonna Forman, 265–80. London: Routledge.

Polanyi, Michael. 1962. *Personal Knowledge: Towards a Post-Critical Philosophy.* London: Routledge.

CHAPTER 7

Smith to Entrepreneurs: Go Forth with Prudence

Kacey Reeves West

Adam Smith's writings leave us with unresolved puzzles. *The Theory of Moral Sentiments* (TMS) cautions us against the dangers of ambition, while the "liberal plan" of *The Wealth of Nations* (WN) gives free reign to certain types of ambition. Scholars continue to explore and debate the contrarieties found in Smith's writings.

There are several puzzles surrounding Smith's thoughts on ambition in economic enterprise and his understanding of entrepreneurship. Some readers say that Smith had little appreciation of entrepreneurship and the dynamism of free markets. Smith balks at the projector who undertakes new projects and endorses the status-quo ceiling on lending at interest, and some take this as evidence of Smith's skeptical attitude toward entrepreneurship. Others, however, have speculated on what Smith says between the lines. Jon Diesel (2021) suggests that Smith dissembled in his endorsement of the interest-rate ceiling, and Dylan DelliSanti (2021) suggests that Smith deliberately downplayed the dynamism of liberalism and therefore obscured the role that entrepreneurship and innovation play in the economy.

Here I treat a related issue: Can the morals of TMS be squared with entrepreneurship? The present essay is based on my article "Prudent Entrepreneurship in *Theory of Moral Sentiments*," published in *Business Ethics Quarterly*. I argue that entrepreneurship can indeed find moral sanction in *TMS*. Furthermore, Smith advises entrepreneurs on how to maintain virtue: Tackle both small and large opportunities with prudence. My argument does not involve claims of esotericism on Smith's part, but like the articles by Diesel and DelliSanti my argument tries to resolve Smithian puzzles surrounding ambition.

The projector vs. the prudent man: Who is the entrepreneur?

Although Smith certainly criticizes the projector, it is not because the projector takes entrepreneurial risk. Rather, it is because the projector foolishly risks squandering social resources. At *WN* 315.74, Smith criticizes projectors for the "distress" that they bring "upon themselves and upon their countr[ies]." Yet because the projector stands as the most obvious reference to the entrepreneur in Smith's works, scholars have assumed that Smith's distaste for the projector translates to a distaste for entrepreneurship (e.g. Campbell and Skinner 1976; Rashid 1988; McCloskey 2016). But such an interpretation tends to assume that entrepreneurs universally resemble the impulsive, "chimerical" projector (*WN* 316.77).

That leads us to an important question: What is entrepreneurship? One approach identifies entrepreneurship by new-venture creation, holding: "entrepreneurs create organizations, while non-entrepreneurs do not" (Gartner 1988, 11). Another, the "trait approach," highlights personal characteristics, like age, manner, attitudes, and risk tolerance (Howell 1972; Brockhaus and Horwitz 1986). Meanwhile, William Baumol (1990; 2010) argued that entrepreneurship can take the form of many different activities and that entrepreneurs bear little resemblance to each other. Saras Sarasvathy (2001; 2008) expands on Baumol to present a model of effectual decision-making. And other theorists have variously associated entrepreneurship with creating, imagining, owning, bearing uncertainty, discovering opportunity, leading and persuading, and so on.

Let's see whether the facets of entrepreneurship can be squared with a character in *TMS* who, at first glance, seems to have little to do with entrepreneurship. In Part VI, Smith presents a character sketch of the prudent man. Unlike the projector, the prudent man is cautious, dependable, and modest. These character traits alone might seem to exclude the prudent person from any definition of entrepreneurship rooted in the trait approach. Yet Smith takes care to show that the prudent person is willing to take risks, as long as those risks are apprehended with care. Smith writes:

> [The prudent man] has no anxiety to change so comfortable a situation, and does not go in quest of new enterprises and adventures, which might endanger, but could not well increase, the secure tranquility which he actually enjoys. *If he enters into any new projects or enterprises, they are likely to be well concerted and prepared.* He can never be hurried or drove into them by any necessity, *but has always time and leisure to deliberate soberly and coolly* concerning what are likely to be their consequences. (215.12, emphasis added)

Smith also takes care to show that the prudent person's actions are virtuous and well-regarded by others. He praises prudent persons for receiving constant support from the impartial spectator and notes that the virtue of prudence serves as a basis for excellent conduct (*TMS* 215.11, 216.14). And notice that Smith says the prudent man deliberates "soberly"—in WN (357.15) Smith indicates that "sober" is exactly what projectors were not.

The prudent man, then, not only has the capacity to resemble an entrepreneur in his ability to "locate new ideas and put them into effect" (Baumol 1968, 65), but also receives approbation in the Smithian moral framework. Acknowledging that the prudent person can be an entrepreneur underscores that Smith's beef with the projector is not that he launches new projects but that he launches new projects in an imprudent manner. We can think of Smith as anticipating Baumol's (1990) distinction between productive and destructive entrepreneurs.

Two principles for moral entrepreneurship

My argument that the prudent man can serve as an example of productive entrepreneurship in Smith's works finds support in *TMS* Part III, Chap. IV, in which Smith lays out a moral framework for the pursuit of wealth, career, or legacy. Smith's framework consists of two principles:

> *Principle 1*: Pursue small matters not with tumultuous passion but with the general "tenor of conduct" that governs your life and trade (TMS 172.6).

> *Principle 2*: Pursue large matters with earnest ambition that is bound by both prudence and justice (TMS 173-4.7).

When we consider these principles in the context of business and trade, it becomes clear that Smith views prudence as a necessary ingredient for moral conduct in enterprise. Prudence should be thought of as a prerequisite to "sober" entrepreneurship; it is a hinderance only to enterprising without sobriety.

The first principle, which relates less to entrepreneurship, concerns routine decisions that do not drastically alter the course of one's life but rather influence one's livelihood as they add up over time. We can think of a baker who owns his own shop. If a vulnerable traveler walks in and asks to buy a loaf of bread, the baker can either sell the loaf of bread for its usual price or overcharge the ignorant traveler. Although the "miser" who is "anxious in small matters for their own sake" would overcharge the traveler for the bread, the person of "exact oeconomy and assiduity" would not alter his behavior but rather preserve the "scheme of life which he has laid down to himself" and treat the traveler as he would any normal customer (*TMS* 173.6). The person of "exact oeconomy and assiduity" does so because he recognizes that acting virtuously—and thus maintaining a reputation as a shopkeeper who acts virtuously—is worth more than the chance to earn an extra shilling. As Smith elaborates in *Lectures on Jurisprudence* (LJ):

> [W]herever dealings are frequent, a man does not expect to
> gain so much by any one contract as by probity and punc-
> tuality in the whole, and a *prudent dealer*, who is sensible
> of his real interest, would rather chuse to lose what he has
> a right to than give any ground for suspicion. (539.328,
> emphasis added)

Thus, the first principle reveals that prudence is a necessary ingredient for everyday business dealings.

The second principle concerns big decisions that can drastically alter the course of one's life in a single moment, and relates more to entrepreneurship. By no means does Smith say that people should steer away from big opportunities. Indeed, Smith writes that if a person does not strive to take advantage of an "extraordinary job" that presents itself to her, she will be considered a "poor-spirited fellow" by her peers (*TMS*

173.7). But Smith advises that we should approach big opportunities differently than we approach routine decisions.

Smith cautions that these life-changing opportunities might tempt individuals to abandon virtue and embrace vice. For that reason, Smith calls on individuals to tackle life-changing opportunities with prudence and justice lest they fall prey to disordered ambition:

> Those great objects of self-interest, of which the loss or acquisition quite changes the rank of the person, are the objects of the passion properly called ambition; a passion, *which when it keeps within the bound of prudence and justice, is always admired in the world*, and has even sometimes a certain irregular greatness, which dazzles the imagination, when it passes the limits of both these virtues, and is not only unjust but extravagant. Hence the general admiration for heroes and conquerors, and even for statesmen, whose *projects* have been very daring and extensive, though altogether devoid of justice... (*TMS* 173.7, emphasis added)

Here, the virtue of prudence takes center stage. If the entrepreneur does not practice prudence in his pursuit of a new business advantage, he risks becoming a destructive projector. The passage also underscores how the virtue of prudence itself is distinct from the prudent man. Whereas the prudent man might not seek out big opportunities, or even hesitate to take them on, the virtue of prudence is still necessary for the pursuit of large entrepreneurial undertakings.

Localism and prudence

Smith tells us to undertake big decisions with prudence and justice. But what does that mean as a practical matter? Smith gives pertinent examples at *TMS* 173.7, where he writes of the prince who wages battle to protect his nation, a member of parliament who competes to win a reelection, and a businessman who strives to obtain an uncommon advantage. The common thread in these examples is that the object of each character's pursuit aligns with his livelihood. The prince tends to his own matters, as does the businessman. Neither party attempts to meddle in affairs that are not his own—it would be imprudent for them to do so.

These examples are significant because they underscore the important theme of localism in Smith's work. Smith recognizes that individuals do not have an unlimited capacity to sympathize with others, nor do we have unlimited power to do good. Rather, individuals naturally face geographical and relational constraints. We sympathize with what is focal to us, such as a problem in our community, more easily than with what is not focal to us, such as a problem in a community in a foreign country (Matson 2022). Smith teaches that individuals should embrace their natural limitations and focus on accomplishing what is in their control— cooking dinner for their family—rather than what is not in their control—solving world hunger. Smith's intention is not to endorse clannish or self-centered behavior, but rather to push us to take action on matters where our efforts are effective (Forman-Barzilai 2010, 22).

The theme of localism also surfaces in the discussion of the prudent man and the projector. While the projector chases far-off opportunities that he has little knowledge of, the prudent person "does not go in quest" of new opportunities (*TMS* 215.12). Rather, the prudent person's deep expertise of her trade allows her to remain alert to new opportunities and judge them without becoming deluded by vain ambition. In some cases, the prudent person's proximity to her work also acts as an incentive for her to continue practicing prudence. Contrast the "prudent dealer" of *LJ* 539.328 with the director of a joint stock company that Smith mentions in *WN* 741.18. Whereas the prudent dealer's position as the residual claimant incentivizes her to handle transactions with honesty and probity, the limited liability held by the director incentivizes him to handle transactions with "negligence and profusion" (*LJ* 539.328).

There is a key relationship between prudence and proximity: The deep knowledge of an individual's trade that comes only when she dedicates her full attention to what is at hand, rather than the politics of "clubs and cabals" (*TMS* 13.7), is necessary for prudent decision-making.

Takeaways for the modern entrepreneur

I do not draw prudent entrepreneurship out of Smith's writings to suggest that the modern entrepreneur should adopt a series of strict rules, but rather that she consider how prudence or localism might be relevant to her affairs. After all, Smith wrote in the tradition of virtue ethics which sought to offer "loose, vague, and indeterminate" guidelines as opposed to exact rules (*TMS* 175.11). The two principles set out above are vague in nature. And their application depends heavily on circumstances. Smith wrote at a time when business was stifled by social and political constraints. That remains true today, but in different ways. Each entrepreneur faces a world of challenges and opportunities, and that world is always changing.

We find in Smith both condemnation of imprudent projectors and endorsement of prudent entrepreneurs. Although projectors occasionally turn a profit, it comes at the risk of squandering resources and missing out on more sober opportunities. And although prudent persons sometimes suffer losses, their careful planning often mitigates the effects on others. That Smith understands entrepreneurs to receive approbation from the impartial spectator based on their motives, as opposed to their balance sheets, reveals that Smith is concerned with the total effect that an entrepreneurial venture has on society. For Smith, the world is complex, and our sense-making grows complicated. In going forth, entrepreneurs should proceed creatively but, above all, prudently.

References

Baumol, William J. 1968. Entrepreneurship in Economic Theory. *The American Economic Review* 58(2): 64-71.

Baumol, William J. 1990. Entrepreneurship: Productive, Unproductive, and Destructive. *Journal of Political Economy* 98(5): 893-921.

Baumol, William J. 2010. *The Microtheory of Innovative Entrepreneurship*. Princeton: Princeton University Press.

Brockhaus, Robert H. and Pamela S. Horwitz. 1986. The Psychology of the Entrepreneur. In *The Art and Science of Entrepreneurship*, ed. R. W. Smilor, 25-48. Cambridge: Ballinger.

Diesel, Jonathon. 2021. Adam Smith on Usury: An Esoteric Reading. *Journal of Economic Behavior and Organization* 184: 727-738.

DelliSanti, Dylan. 2021. The Dynamism of Liberalism: An Esoteric Interpretation of Adam Smith. *Journal of Economic Behavior and Organization* 184: 717-726.

Forman-Borzilai, Fonna. 2010. *Adam Smith and the Circles of Sympathy: Cosmopolitanism and Moral Theory*. Cambridge: Cambridge University Press.

Gartner, William B. 1988. "Who Is an Entrepreneur?" Is the Wrong Question. *American Journal of Small Business* 13 (2): 11-32.

Howell, Richard P. 1972. Comparative Profiles: Entrepreneurs Versus the Hired Executive: San Francisco Peninsula Semiconductor Industry. In *Technical Entrepreneurship: A Symposium*, eds. A. C. Cooper and J. L. Komives, 47-62. Milwaukee: Center for Venture Management.

Matson, Erik. 2022. The Edifying Discourses of Adam Smith: Focalism, Commerce, and Serving the Common Good. *Journal of the History of Economic Thought* 42(2): 298-320.

McCloskey, Deirdre. 2016. *Bourgeois Equality: How Ideas, Not Capital or Institutions, Enriched the World*. Chicago: University of Chicago Press.

Rashid, Salim. 1998. *The Myth of Adam Smith*. Cheltenham: Edward Elgar Publishing.

Sarasvathy, Saras D. 2001. Causation and Effectuation: Toward a Theoretical Shift from Economic Inevitability to Entrepreneurial Contingency. *The Academy of Management Review* 26 (2): 243-263.

Sarasvathy, Saras D. 2008. *Effectuation: Elements of Entrepreneurial Expertise*. Cheltenham: Edward Elgar Publishing.

Smith, Adam. 1982 [1776]. *An Inquiry into the Nature and Causes of the Wealth of Nations*, eds. R.H. Campbell and A.S. Skinner. 2 vols. Indianapolis: Liberty Fund.

Smith, Adam. 1982. *Lectures on Jurisprudence*, eds. R. L. Meek, D. D. Raphael, and P. G. Stein. Indianapolis: Liberty Fund.

Smith, Adam. 1982 [1759]. *The Theory of Moral Sentiments*, eds. D.D. Raphael and A.L. Macfie. Indianapolis: Liberty Fund.

West, Kacey Reeves. 2024. Prudent Entrepreneurship in *Theory of Moral Sentiments*. *Business Ethics Quarterly* 34(1): 129-162.

CHAPTER 8

Essential Words in—and Not in— Adam Smith's Essential Works

Caleb Petitt and Daniel B. Klein

The word *sympathy* (and its cognates) appears 290 times in Adam Smith's *The Theory of Moral Sentiments* (TMS). In a letter to Smith (28 July 1759), David Hume said that the agreeableness of sympathy is "the Hinge" of Smith's entire moral theory. Yet in Smith's subsequent and much longer work, *The Wealth of Nations* (WN), the number of times that 'sympathy' appears is zero. Consider that: 290 in TMS, 0 in WN. It is impossible not to see that as a conscious, deliberate choice by the author. And it raises the question: Is Smith's moral hinge absent from WN?

Consider the word *sentiment* (and its cognates). There are 333 appearances in TMS. Yet that word appears only twice in WN. Likewise, 'spectator,' abundant in TMS, occurs only twice in WN.

TABLE 1: NUMBER OF OCCURRENCES OF TERMS, IN TMS AND IN WN

Root Searched	"sympath"	"beneficen"	"amiabl"	"sentiment"	"spectator"	"compassion"	"conscience"	"virtu"	"benevolen"	"temperan"	"friendship"	"enter into"	"pruden"	"charit"
TMS	290	53	44	333	163	36	21	402	77	21	44	90	81	10
WN	0	0	0	2	2	1	1	20	4	3	8	17	51	15

Methods: Read the footnote.[1]

There is a very clear shift in the language used by Smith in his two great works. Table 1 lists words that are characteristic of TMS. Those words speak of the individual's sentimental endeavor to make sense of her social world and her place in it. They speak of her path upward in wisdom and virtue. In TMS, the human being is viewed with inner intricacy. There is an intimacy. That inner intricacy is quite absent in WN. When one passes from reading TMS to reading WN, one notices a striking shift away from the warm sense of human relations, aspirations, and the inner call to virtue, to a cooler, more distant treatment of social processes and social mechanisms. That the words listed in Table 1 are so little used in WN—2.6 times the length of TMS—is truly striking.

The shift is well-known to Smith scholars, and it speaks to the relationship between TMS and WN. The consensus of Smith scholarship today, with which we concur, is that there is just one Adam Smith, even if the two works differ in feeling and perspective. Indeed, a dialectical mixing of perspectives happens within a famous passage

---

1. HTML copies of WN and TMS on the Liberty Fund website were searched for the word counts. Search results for TMS include results from the Essay on Languages. The root searched column shows the text searched for. Searching for the roots helped capture different variations of a word in a single search, such as sympathy and sympathize from "sympath". The TMS and WN column exclude any results from the editor's introduction or the editor's footnotes. 'Virtually' was excluded from search results coming from "virtu," and 'jurisprudence' was removed from "pruden". An Excel file of the data is available upon request.

of TMS, the parable of the poor man's son, where a "splenetic" perspective is followed by a perspective of "better health and better humour" (TMS 183.9). There's nothing inconsistent about an author developing differing feelings or perspectives.

Perhaps the shift is best understood as involving, first, a change in topics, that is, a change in the issues and affairs treated. With that change comes a second, a change in perspective, that is, a change in how one regards human conduct—a change in the lens used in contemplating social affairs. Finally, those two changes seem to be joined with a deliberate stylistic decision to sustain the shift quite systematically.

In TMS, Smith develops moral theory in a way that keeps the agreeableness of sympathy the central hinge. In WN, Smith develops political economy: he takes the purposes of any given individual at a distance, and goes from there. The implicit lessons are that beyond the intimacy of relational knowledge, we cannot much know the deeper springs of the individual's purposes. Political economy—"the science of a statesman or legislator" (WN, 428.1)—cannot hope much to instruct or engineer the deeper springs of those purposes. Compared to voluntary corrective measures and social feedback offered by friends, family, colleagues, and customers, the manipulations of public policy are blunt, like taking a hammer to the intricate workings inside a watch. And, the manipulations of public policy are, as Smith continually reminds us in WN, highly subject to greed, folly, and superstition.

The only word in Table 1 used more often in WN than in TMS is *charity*. But WN is much longer than TMS. To adjust for length, we multiply the term frequencies for TMS by 2.6, as WN is 950 pages in the modern Glasgow edition (OUP/Liberty Fund), and TMS is 366 pages (we include the Language essay as part of TMS), and 950/366 is approximately 2.6. The rightmost column in Table 2 shows the ratio, adjusted for length.

TABLE 2: RATIO ADJUSTING FOR BOOK LENGTH

Root Searched	TMS*2.6	WN	Ratio: TMS*2.6/WN
"sympath"	754	0	infinite
"beneficen"	137.8	0	infinite
"amiabl"	114.4	0	infinite
"sentiment"	865.8	2	432.9
"spectator"	423.8	2	211.9
"compassion"	93.6	1	93.6
"conscience"	54.6	1	54.6
"virtu"	1045.2	20	52.26
"benevolen"	200.2	4	50.05
"temperan"	54.6	3	18.2
"friendship"	114.4	8	14.3
"enter into"	234	17	13.8
"pruden"	210.6	51	4.1
"charit"	26	15	1.7

Difference between TMS and WN in word usage is also seen in TMS's heavy use of musical and synchrony metaphors such as *harmony*, *pitch*, *concord*, *discord*, and *keep time with*, yet slight in WN. Klein and Clark (2011) provide a count of such terms that dovetails with the tables above.

Smith's unified discourse

Man's ability to sympathize with others is constrained by knowledge. The more that someone knows about another's situation the more completely she can enter into the other's sentiments. People desire sympathy, but for people to be able to enter into a person's sentiments, that person must lower "his passion to that pitch...which the spectators are capable of going along with" (TMS 22.7).

Further, people adjust the pitch of their passions based on how close they are to the spectator. It is harder for strangers to sympathize with one another than for close friends to sympathize with one another. As Smith says, "We expect still less sympathy from an assembly of strangers, and we assume, therefore, still more tranquility before them, and always endeavour to bring down our passion to that pitch, which the particular company we are in may be expected to go along with" (TMS 23.9).

The account of sympathy that Smith gives in TMS should prepare the reader to expect works like WN to take people's purposes as we seem to find them, and as they themselves frankly present them in transactions. We do not appeal to benevolence to get our dinner from the butcher, baker, or brewer. However, we can expect a ride to the airport from a friend or family member by appealing to their benevolence. The difference in how appeals are made is not the result of a schizophrenic understanding of human nature, but rather knowledge that different sentiments prevail depending on the nature of a given relationship. J.R. Clark and Dwight Lee (2017) discuss what they call the amiable morality of TMS as opposed to the mundane morality of WN.

Smith saw WN as an extension of TMS. In the final paragraph of TMS, Smith announces that he "shall in another discourse endeavour to give an account of the general principles of law and government, and of the different revolutions of society, not only in that which concerns justice, but in what concerns police, revenue, and arms, and whatever else is the object of law" (TMS 342.37). In the 1790 preface to TMS, Smith confirms that he thought of WN as completing his promise to give an account for what concerns policy, revenue, and arms.

The connection between TMS and WN can be understood in terms of Smith's four sources of moral approval. When we consider the action by some fellow, call him Jim, we consider four sorts of viewpoints. The first three are more micro in nature: (1) sympathy/antipathy with Jim's motives and intentions, (2) gratitude/resentment with those whom Jim acts upon, and (3) the alignment of Jim's conduct with established rules and expectations for interaction between Jim and such others. But the final source throws things wide open, to macro ramifications: (4) The "taste for beauty and order which is excited by inanimate as well as animated objects" (TMS 327.16). The taste for beauty and order excited by objects is a large part of what Smith is trying to develop in the readers of WN.

WN continues to instruct us in virtue. The chief action that Smith is trying to improve is the readers' estimation of ideas and judgments in economics and political economy. Those objects of estimation are social processes involving many people about whom we know very little. But the program remains one of virtue—a program in estimating objects properly.

In the opening passages of WN, Smith appeals to the taste for beauty and order in the division of labor in the pin factory. Smith then extends the appreciation to activities "from the remotest corners of the world!" (WN 23.11) that make the woolen coat. Our appreciation of that immense concatenation lacks the visible scene of a factory floor. People participating in the immensity can be thought of communicating and cooperating with one another only metaphorically. Each person's inner moral springs are unknown to us analysts and almost all of those who take part in the immense concatenation.

The full title of TMS presents the book as focused on the principles by which men judge their neighbors and themselves: "*The Theory of Moral Sentiments, or An Essay towards an Analysis of the Principles by which Men naturally judge concerning the Conduct and Character, first of their Neighbours, and afterwards of themselves.*" There is more about politics than that full title suggests, and some of it may be between the lines. But for the most part the reader of TMS is left to wonder how citizens should judge the rules laid down by rulers. In WN Smith treats the principles by which men can judge the character and conduct of governors.

WN's rare 'spectators' and 'sentiments'

Smith uses 'spectator' only twice in WN: in the second paragraph of the first chapter, and in the third-to-last paragraph of the entire book. The 'spectator' bookending of WN is plainly deliberate.

The first 'spectator' is in the pin factory: "those employed in every different branch of the work can often be collected into the same workhouse, and under the view of the spectator" (WN 15.2). The second comes while Smith addresses how people get caught up in faction. Those of distant provinces are less likely to get caught up in the factional ambitions that run rampant within the heart of the empire. The distances "makes them enter less into the views of any of the contending parties, and renders them more indifferent and impartial spectators of the conduct of all" (WN 945.90).

As for WN's two uses of 'sentiment,' one returns to the scene of division of labor on the factory floor. Smith portrays the moral effects of narrow specialization. He describes the man who is employed in a simple, monotonous task as becoming not only dull and ignorant, but incapable of "conceiving any generous, noble, or tender sentiment" (WN 782.50). Smith does not present his readers with a one-sided view of the effects of industrial life, but instead provides a balanced presentation, and uses the term *sentiment* to draw attention to the various moral effects of market activity.

WN's other use of 'sentiment' comes in Smith's analysis of teachers who earn a significant part of their salaries through fees from their students. Some teachers, he says, are concerned for their reputation, which depends on "the affection, gratitude, and favorable report of those who have attended his instructions; and these favourable sentiments he is likely to gain in no way so well as by deserving them" (WN 760.6). Here Smith highlights how market activity can move people toward virtue.

The dramatic difference in the language used by Smith in his two books does not reflect a change in Smith over time. The last great achievement of Smith's life was revising and expanding TMS, enhancing its inner richness. The additions in 1790 included "Of Universal Benevolence," in which Smith squares duty to universal benevolence with attention to life's focal matters, as effectiveness in acting beneficially to the whole depends on knowledge, and your focal matters are part of the whole (Matson provides more on Smith, universal benevolence, and focalism in Chapter 4). The language shift is all part of a larger, coherent, unified attempt to improve people's judgments.

Smith does not treat the intricacies of the souls of the actors in WN. WN treats social forces in a de-personalized language. It uses generalizations such as labour, price, rent, speculation, capital, and profit. It speaks of markets in land, wool, corn, and pots and pans.

So, don't leave TMS behind when reading WN. Intricate souls the actors in WN surely are. What, after all, is the inner substance of the wealth of nations? In WN, Smith describes the true meaning of the wealth of nations:

> [I]f the quantity of victuals were to increase, the number of pots and pans would readily increase along with it... [T]he quantity of plate is regulated by the number and wealth of those private families who chuse to indulge themselves in that sort of magnificence: increase the number and wealth of such families, and a part of this increased wealth will most probably be employed in purchasing, wherever it is to be found, an additional quantity of plate: that to attempt to increase the wealth of any country, either by introducing or by detaining in it an unnecessary quantity of gold and silver, is as absurd as it would be to attempt to increase the good cheer of private families, by obliging them to keep an unnecessary number of kitchen utensils. (439-40.19)

References

Clark, J. R., and Dwight R. Lee. 2017. Econ 101 Morality: The Amiable, the Mundane, and the Market. *Econ Journal Watch* 14(1): 61-76.

Klein, Daniel B., and Michael J. Clark. (2011). The Music of Social Intercourse: Synchrony in Adam Smith. *The Independent Review* 15(3), 413–420.

Smith, Adam. 1982 [1776]. *An Inquiry into the Nature and Causes of the Wealth of Nations*, eds. R.H. Campbell and A.S. Skinner. 2 vols. Indianapolis: Liberty Fund.

Smith, Adam. 1982 [1759]. *The Theory of Moral Sentiments*, eds. D.D. Raphael and A.L. Macfie. Indianapolis: Liberty Fund.

CHAPTER 9

Adam Smith's Space Odyssey

Erik W. Matson

S mith developed an essay over the course of his career, published posthumously, now commonly abbreviated as "History of Astronomy" (HA). The abbreviated title facilitates a misapprehension. The history of astronomy is, in some sense, auxiliary; it is a vehicle with which Smith develops ideas about the nature of the scientific or philosophic enterprise itself. The essay's full title makes this clear: "An Inquiry into the Principles which Lead and Direct Philosophical Enquiries; Illustrated by the History of Astronomy."

HA, we find, is an adventure into reflection on the passional and aesthetic dimensions of scientific and philosophic practice. The essay teaches us something important about Smith's rhetorical method and his ideas of the deeply personal nature of knowledge.

Teaching by showing

Donald Livingston describes David Hume as an essentially dialectical thinker. By this he means that for Hume, "philosophical insight is gained by working through the contrarieties of thought which structure a drama of inquiry" (Livingston 1984, 35). This description of Hume's method can be used to characterize important moments in Smith's work. One such moment is the parable in the *Theory of Moral*

Sentiments of "the poor man's son" (Smith 1982b [hereater 'TMS'], 181). The poor man's son sets out with wrongheaded ambitions that lead him to effectively pursue his own unhappiness. But his actions, Smith contends, have unintended beneficial consequences for humankind, leading him and his trading partners to "cultivate the ground, to build houses, to found cities and commonwealths, and to invent and improve all the arts and sciences" (TMS, 183). In the juxtaposition of these perspectives, which culminate in the first published "invisible hand" passage in Smith's work, Smith, as I've argued elsewhere, "actively encourages the reader to reflect upon how the pursuits of wealth and happiness [can be] balanced and complementary, not oppositional modes of life" (Matson 2021, 834). Smith works to convey something about the relationship between commercial pursuits and the good life, in other words, not simply through explication, but by drawing the reader into a progression of sentiment.

This rhetorical method of teaching by showing looms large in Smith's ethics. As Charles Griswold puts the point, in TMS Smith "focuses our attention on particulars and experience and attempts to get us to 'see' things in a certain light rather than simply to argue us into accepting a philosophical position" (Griswold 1999, 829). We learn the look and feel of proper moral judgment by observing the enactment of moral judgment throughout Smith's prose. A similar rhetorical method is essential to the dramatic arc of "History of Astronomy." HA attempts to teach us something about the personal dimensions of knowledge and the sentimental nature of the scientific process not simply by explanation, but by ostension—that is, showing the process. Smith offers the reader a drama, a progression of sentiment.

Passion for regularity

HA begins with a treatment of three sentiments that give rise to philosophy: wonder, surprise, and admiration, characterized as follows. "We wonder at all extraordinary and uncommon objects"; "we are surprised at those things which we have seen often, but which we least of all expect to meet with in the place where we find them"; and "we admire the beauty of a plain or the greatness of a mountain" (EPS 33). Underneath these sentiments lies a natural belief, one that all human beings instinctively accept and which must be taken for granted in all our reasonings. This belief is the assumption that reality proceeds uniformly in accordance with rules.

Smith seems to follow Hume in admitting that we have no way to demonstrate that reality is in fact regular and uniform (Matson 2019). Our natural belief in causal relations, and even in the enduring existence of the objects of sensory experience, is vulnerable to skeptical criticism. But our passion for coherence, our conviction that irregularities could be accounted for with fuller accounts of reality, wins the day over skeptical pause. Hume writes, "thus the sceptic still continues to reason and believe, even tho' he asserts, that he cannot defend his reason by reason" (Hume 2007, 125). The mind displays a deep commitment to the idea of regularity; skepticism is rendered ineffectual not by ratiocination, but by the natural strength of our conviction that the world makes some kind of sense, even if we lack enough knowledge to participate in its apprehension. (Reports of Hume's skepticism have been greatly exaggerated.)

Within our natural belief in regularity, philosophy, Smith tells us, is essentially an effort of imagination to impose the greatest possible degree of order and coherence upon the chaos of experience. We experiment with various interpretations to render the "theatre of nature a more coherent, and therefore a more magnificent spectacle, than it otherwise would appear" (EPS, 46). We are temporarily jarred out of our current interpretative framework by the sentiment of surprise, caused by unexpected observations and experiences. If we cannot find a way to accommodate such surprises by "enlarg[ing] the precincts" (EPS, 40) of our framework, we feel wonder. And wonder, Smith says, impels us to reimagine the way things are and to engage in a process of generating new modes of explanation—potentially bringing discovery.

Although it receives in HA much less explicit attention than surprise and wonder (both have dedicated subsections in the essay), admiration enters the philosophic process at various points. Two are worth mentioning here. First, admiration affects how the knowledge-seeker allocates his attention, guiding him towards grand and beautiful objects, such as the celestial heavens or the breathtaking concatenation of human activities comprising the modern economy. Second, admiration recommends to him remarkable men and women worthy of emulation in his ponderings, like Isaac Newton. In TMS, Smith writes, "it is the great leader in science and taste, the man who directs and conducts our own sentiments...who excites our admiration, and seems to deserve our applause" (TMS, 20). Admiration inspires the effort to understand and enter into great minds; that effort is an essential part of the cultivation of intellect and the practice of philosophy. (Reports on the dispensability of great minds of the past have been greatly exaggerated.)

HA as drama of inquiry

After surprise, wonder, and admiration, astronomy appears on the scene. The history of astronomy is framed as a case study in the role of the intellectual passions in the scientific process. In transitioning to this case study, Smith makes an important caveat. He tells the reader that he intends to treat systems of astronomy not as explanations of reality, but as inventions of the imagination to satisfy the mind's desire for order and tranquility (EPS, 46). This statement of intent is the first key moment in HA's drama of inquiry.

In the earlier part of his account of the history of astronomy, treating the progression from Aristotelean to Ptolemaic to Cartesian astronomy, Smith emphasizes—in keeping with his stated intentions—the passional, aesthetic, and sociological aspects of what those thinkers said, rather than emphasizing their theorizing as better or worse approximations of reality. Such systems are treated as in or out of "vogue" (EPS, 63), as relieving the imagination from embarrassment (EPS, 62), and advancing on the basis of "beauty and simplicity" (EPS, 75).

As the essay unfolds, however, Smith appears to have trouble keeping his distance from the ambition to know reality. He slips towards the common treatment of scientific explanations not just as systems fitted to sooth the mind, but as attempts to describe reality. The slippage becomes pronounced in his treatment of Newton.

In the final paragraph of the essay, Smith abruptly takes notice of the progression within his own thinking. He realizes his departure from his announced plan. He has failed to treat theories of astronomy merely as efforts to render the theater of nature agreeable and coherent. He has been led—unavoidably, it seems—to view Newton's system not just as the latest, most agreeable system, but as an explanation of the world as it actually is. He explicitly calls attention to his failure, such as it is, in the final words of the essay:

> And even we, while we have been endeavouring to represent all philosophical systems as mere inventions of the imagination, to connect together the otherwise disjointed and discordant phaenomena of nature, have insensibly been drawn in, to make use of language expressing the connecting principles of this one, as if they were the real chains

which Nature makes use of to bind together her several
operations. Can we wonder then, that [Newton's system]
should have gained the general and complete approbation
of mankind, and that it should now be considered, not as
an attempt to connect in the imagination the phaenomena
of the Heavens, but as the greatest discovery that ever was
made by man, the discovery of an immense chain of the
most important and sublime truths, all closely connected
together, by one capital fact, of the reality of which we have
daily experience. (EPS, 105)

This delightful passage marks the second key moment in HA's
drama of inquiry. Smith praises the principle of gravity, "one capital
fact, of the reality of which we have daily experience," that made possible Newton's integration of the sublunar and the heavenly. He simultaneously intimates a second "capital fact," which is the true discovery
of his odyssey: the mind can't escape its ambition to know and explain
reality, and to view its deepest theories as truth.

Pondering Smith's contrariety

The two key moments of Smith's drama together make a contrariety,
which we can now express with the following propositions:

1. Philosophical systems can be treated as inventions of
    the imagination, fitted to sooth the human passion
    for regularity and coherence. (EPS, 46)

2. We cannot avoid but treat the philosophical systems
    to which we adhere as real accounts of the workings
    of the universe. (EPS, 105)

Smith invites us to ponder the contrariety. He does so by expressing—and thus invoking in us, his sympathetic readers—the three sentiments he described earlier as giving rise to philosophy. We feel surprised upon observing Smith's surprise at his subconscious slide towards realism. We wonder as Smith wonders at the power and beauty of Newton's philosophy. And we admire with Smith the singularity of Newton's genius.

As we participate in Smith's passions, we can't help but feel still higher levels of surprise, wonder, and admiration: surprise at the ending of Smith's essay, wonder at the novelty of his ironic self-contradiction, and admiration for *his* genius. The sentiments encourage us to puzzle over Smith's contrariety and arrive at a fuller sense of the purpose of his essay.

In Matson (2019) I suggested that Smith uses the contrariety to develop HA into something like a rhetorical exercise in Humean naturalism. In developing the sentimental and aesthetic aspects of inquiry, Smith admits that our natural beliefs in causal relations and the existence of objects outside of our field of sensory experience are unverifiable through reason alone, and, from that observation, skepticism can ensue. But, if our idea of what we call causation derives from repeated association of objects (see EPS, 40-41), what knowledge can we have of true causal relations? Such skepticism is unstable, however, and Smith illustrates its instability through his own personal progress of sentiment throughout HA. Smith shows the reader the process by which the mind naturally gravitates towards belief formation by going through the process himself. In showing how he is unable to keep to his intent of treating all scientific systems with a degree of distance, Smith intimates something about the psychological robustness of our beliefs in our own explanations.

In 2019, I characterized the overarching message of HA in this way: "if unverifiable belief dominates an investigation into the very principles directing scientific or philosophical inquiry, then such unverifiable belief should be understood to subconsciously constitute science more generally" (Matson 2019, 266). I now think this characterization somewhat misses the mark. The phrase "unverifiable belief" misconstrues the main point I believe Smith seeks to convey. Smith is not agnostic on the truth-value of various scientific systems, which some parts of Matson (2019) seem to suggest. The larger point, I believe, is that Smith sees that truth is not received passively, but engaged with, actively and personally, and that such engagement requires commitment, in the sense of that concept advanced by Michael Polanyi (1962).

Commitment amounts to "the affirmation of personal convictions with universal intent" (Polanyi 1962, 341). Only from within a personal commitment can we comment on the truth or untruth of a philosophical interpretation. I now think that it is something along these lines that Smith's drama of inquiry looks to convey. Even in the face of our admission of room for potential future improvement, even in the face of our own reflections on the sociological and aesthetic dimensions of scientific and philosophical practice, we can't help but profess our convictions of truth, based on our deepest-to-date modes of understanding. Even in the face of his extensive consideration of the passional and social elements of the scientific process, Smith, apparently, can't help but treat Newton as exceptional, as the standard by which truthfulness of a system of astronomy is to be measured.

Smith calls attention to his own commitments and the way they've shaped his assessment of the history of astronomy, despite his apparent intentions. He intimates something to the reader about his views on the irreducibly personal and passional nature of inquiry. To rephrase my 2019 characterization, then: if personal commitment dominates an investigation into the very principles directing scientific or philosophical inquiry, then such commitment should be understood to pervade scientific and philosophical practice generally. HA does not convey an anti-realist attitude about the truth-value of scientific explanations; rather, it conveys a passional, sentimental conception of scientific practice, along with a personal conception of how one apprehends truth itself.

References

Griswold, Charles L. 1999. *Adam Smith and the Virtues of Enlightenment*. New York: Cambridge University Press.

Hume, David. 2007. *A Treatise of Human Nature*, eds. David F. Norton and Mary J. Norton. 2 vols. Oxford: Oxford University Press.

Livingston, Donald W. 1984. *Hume's Philosophy of Common Life*. Chicago: University of Chicago Press.

Matson, Erik W. 2019. Adam Smith's Humean Attitude Towards Science; Illustrated by 'The History of Astronomy.' In *The Adam Smith Review: Volume 11*, ed. Fonna Forman, 265–80. London: Routledge.

Matson, Erik W. 2021. A Dialectical Reading of Adam Smith on Wealth and Happiness. *Journal of Economic Behavior & Organization* 184: 826–36.

Polanyi, Michael. 1962. *Personal Knowledge: Towards a Post-Critical Philosophy*. London: Routledge.

Smith, Adam. 1982a. *Essays on Philosophical Subjects*, eds. W.P.D. Wightman and J.C. Bryce. Indianapolis: Liberty Fund.

Smith, Adam. 1982b. *The Theory of Moral Sentiments*, eds. D.D. Raphael and A.L. Macfie. Indianapolis: Liberty Fund.

CHAPTER 10

Adam Smith on Polygamy and Kin Networks

Patrick Fitzsimmons

L et us reflect with Adam Smith on the very broad historical requirements for the emergence of stable liberal polities. We are considering the sweep of centuries past and experiences ranging throughout Europe and beyond Europe.

Liberty requires institutions that keep potential oppressors from running rampant. If a despotic ruler is to be kept from subjugating the populace, opposition is required. Opposition may come in many forms, but Smith understood that multilateral opposition to a potential oppressor would provide more opportunities for countervailing forces. Conquerors from elsewhere are one form of oppressor, but the immediate challenge is facing down homegrown despots.

Meanwhile, a desideratum to avoiding great oppression is an institutional arrangement that spells political stability. Without political stability, the opportunities for potential oppressors are abundant, if constantly shifting. The struggle for power in an unstable polity (or wannabe polity) is almost inevitably oppressive. Political stability does not ensure the limitation of oppression, but it is necessary to a measure of liberty.

Borrowing the violence framework from Douglass North, John

Wallis, and Barry Weingast (2009), we may say that in the absence of political stability rents are scooped up by those actors who have the most potential for violence. Actors would invest in violence potential. The product is a society in which actors are not thinking growth or more extensive cooperation, but rather rent-seeking and immediate personal security.

Adam Smith provided several examples of institutions that could conduce to a stable polity with multilateral opposition and resistance to despotism. One is monogamy—which is to say, laws and customs that prohibit polygamy. Monogamy as a social norm stands in opposition to polygamy.

The source is Smith's *Lectures on Jurisprudence* (LJ); the index of the volume indicates 23 pages for *polygamy*: 150–9, 160–1, 166, 167, 171, 172, 173, 442–5, 448, 449. Polygamy features in both sets of lecture notes, which correspond to lectures given at Glasgow between late 1762 and early 1764. As for all of Smith's other materials (including the *Correspondence*), although some contain pertinent material on kin networks, political development, and so on, "monogamy" and "polygamy" never appear in any of them.

In LJ, Smith shows a strong and unequivocal favor for monogamy, believing it to facilitate social and political stability. Indeed, Smith's apparent opposition to legal polygamy, at least within certain historical settings, should be regarded as one his most significant exceptions to the liberty principle. Smith thought that sometimes direct liberty must be sacrificed for overall liberty.

For Smith, monogamy has three advantages over polygamy in fostering political stability:

First, monogamy leads people to socialize and expand their social networks outside the family. Families are tight kin-networks that may present advantages in the face of despotic or irregular power. But tighter kin-networks have also proven to have a negative correlation with democratic institutions (Schulz 2022). Monogamy helps to break down barriers to interaction between non-kin members.

Second, monogamy produces orderly, intergenerational succession in prominent families; prominent and powerful families enable peaceable succession; customs of peaceable succession lead to the emergence of a nobility. Monogamy also provides a focal point for who will be the next king, elevating one potential over another. When the next king is determined ex ante, violence is less likely to break out between potential claimants.

Third, monogamy creates focal points. For Smith, focal points were crucial in order for people to rise in force against a foreign or domestic oppressor. If the people have no focal individuals who stands above the rest, no leaders, they are unable to band together and form a significant counter to the oppressor and his affiliates. The advantages of monogamous succession and focal points relate to Smith's ideas on the legitimacy of children.

Jealous wives and the jealous husband

"Polygamy excites the most violent jealousy, by which domestic peace is destroyed" (LJ 442). Smith focuses on two jealousy problems. The first is jealousy among wives for the attention of their husband. The second is among men. Smith saw both problems as inherent to polygamy. These jealousies destroy the domestic peace of the family and of the society.

The jealousy among the wives of a husband is multifaceted since polygamy presents both "a jealousy of love and a jealousy of interest, and consequently a want of tranquility" (LJ 443). The wives compete for their husband's favor, attention, and resources as "the wives are all rivals and enemies" (LJ 442). Suppose that Jim is married to Maria, Sarah, and other women in a legally permitted polygamous marriage.

Maria would like to monopolize or at least capture as much of Jim's attention as possible. In Maria's eyes, Sarah is a competitor for limited resource, and Smith's lectures give the impression that the women will not share willingly. Maria and Sarah will "do all that they can to supplant their rivals" (LJ 151). There is now disorder in the household as there is unhealthy competition between the women.

The women feel jealousy also towards one another's children. Both Maria and Sarah have children from Jim. Jim's attention is also divided between the very numerous children. When she looks upon Jim's attention, neither Maria nor Sarah will be happy. Maria's affection is for her children, so she would prefer that Jim's attention be more focused on her children. Maria now sees both Sarah and her children as competition and will act to further the interest of her own child. Jealousy between Maria and Sarah not only keeps them from cooperating, but easily turns invidious and mutually antagonistic. It is a source of trouble and anxiety for Jim. He receives no enjoyment from the exercise of his parental affections but is instead filled with vexation (LJ 153). Jim must deal with complaints from both Maria and Sarah as both "measure the affection of the father by her own, between which there is no proportion, as he is divided among 40 or 50 children and hers only among 4 or 5" (LJ 442-43). This is but one reason why men are not happy under polygamy.

Smith notes that women are competing with each other and missing out on potential social networks. But men, too, find disadvantages and social instability under polygamy.

David Hume and Smith pointed out that polygamy, compared to monogamous marriage, no more leaves the husband better off than it does the wives (LJ 153; see Hume *Essays* 184-85). There is the jealousy that Jim feels towards his neighbor Tom. Whereas in a monogamous country, each of the two men may not feel jealousy about his wife, nor suspect her of anything, it is different for polygamous societies. Jim, the polygamist, understands that Maria and Sarah have less reason to be faithful towards him. Maria and Sarah, living "where polygamy takes place…, being in absolute slavery" to Jim (LJ 445), have little interest in his affairs, similar to how a slave of labor has little concern for the affairs of his master. Jim knows that Maria and Sarah lack reason to be faithful to him, so there is a concern that the neighbor, Tom, may corrupt one of the wives. Jim feels jealousy towards Tom and "on account of the inequality betwixt" Jim and his wives "he can have no entertainment at his own house, no opportunity of social improvements" (LJ 443). Jim hides his wives away from Tom, "lest he bring a lover to his numerous wives" (Hume 1985, 185). Jim and Tom are unable to form a bond as their fear of the other corrupting their women is strong (LJ 153). Confident, cooperative relationships between men, between women, and between men and women are all difficult in polygamous societies.

Furthermore, jealousy caused by polygamy incentivizes violence between men. Modern research has shown that polygamy is correlated with higher levels of violent behavior among men (Henrich et al. 2012).

Smith saw that the jealousy of the wives causes disorder. The husband cannot quell the jealousy or rebellion of his wives himself. He resorts to eunuchs (LJ 152). A eunuch, no longer a viable competitor of the man, keeps the wives in line for his employer. In the absence of institutions that reward men for going the path of eunuch, it is a procedure forced on other men. The strongest man may subjugate his peers. Men then hide from each other.

Monogamy and Legitimate Succession

Smith saw monogamy as solving the problems of succession and legitimation, as "the effect of marriage is to legitimate the children" (LJ

447). The protection of liberty and curbing of elite power could not be done without handling the issue. Smith thought that "there should be some persons who are some way distinguished above the rest and who can make head against the oppressions of the king, or head the people when they are in danger of being oppressed by foreign invaders" (LJ 157). Monogamy allows one individual to be elevated above the others. In noble families, the elevated individual, after the father and husband, is the eldest son, destined to take over his father's duties. The father can focus all of his accumulated knowledge and experience on his eldest son, facilitating intergenerational leadership learning.

The eldest prince takes over his father's throne. In baronial families, before they were able to split up land and power among the children, the eldest son received the inheritance. Noble families begin to form around the elevated individuals.

Each noble family acts as a check on the others. The elevated individual acts as a focal point for soldiers to rally around. As long as a focal point is present, noble families pose a counterweight to one another.

Clear succession is difficult if the elevated child is seen as illegitimate. In monogamous marriages, a child is seen as legitimate, so men are incentivized to enter monogamous marriages. Monogamous marriage handles paternal uncertainty and resolves doubts about the man's rightful heirs (Henrich 2016, 146). In polygamous societies, the connection between child and father is scarce and will have no effect (LJ 157) and then there is no definitive son to be followed.

The only type of family that solves the problem is the family of hereditary nobility, specifically a monogamous family of hereditary nobility. If there is no clear monogamous hereditary nobility, half-brothers become rivals. In a polygamous society, the lack of hereditary nobility coupled with a severe distrust between men leads to tyrannical oppression, as the men are "by this means altogether incapacitated to enter into any associations or alliances to revenge themselves on their oppressors, and curb the extravagant power of the government and support their liberties" (LJ 154.33).

The liberty issue

Smith, citing Grotius, said that there is no injustice in polygamy in countries where it is allowed (LJ 150). Thus, we come to the issue of whether prohibiting polygamy violates commutative justice and thus reduces liberty. That issue for polygamy relates to several other kin issues, including whether *restrictions* on incest, marrying among kin, "voluntary divorce," and neglecting one's own children violate commutative justice and hence reduce liberty.

For Smith, when polygamy is allowed and a wife is taken as one of many wives, there is no injury to her when she finds herself in that situation. But while "there is not any injustice in the practise of polygamy where the law permits it, yet it is productive of many bad consequences" (151).

Smith is referring to countries where polygamy is allowed by law. The woman needs to be aware that she is going to be one of many wives. The man must be honest about the terms the woman is agreeing to.

It is my opinion—without getting into the parsing of the matter—that Smith would have supported restrictions on polygamy as an exception to the liberty principle in the direct sense, since Jim, Mary, and Sarah violate no one's person, property, or promises-due when they voluntarily agree to bigamy, and to bring violence against such a voluntary affair is to initiate coercion and violate liberty.

But when it comes to liberty in an indirect or overall way, or ramifications, Smith lays out how monogamy instead of polygamy provides safeguards to a nation's liberty. Smith clearly sees a connection between liberty and monogamy—"polygamy takes place under despotic governments" (LJ 443). Monogamy not only leads to liberty, but liberty may lead to monogamy as "in every country freedom puts out polygamy" (LJ 443).

Concluding remarks

Smith on monogamy versus polygamy relates to the wide considerations of what made possible a modern era of relatively liberal nation-states. The topic treated here relates to restrictions on incest, consanguineous marriages, and divorce, as such regulations, too, would be regarded by Smith as exceptions to the direct-liberty principle, but favorable to liberty overall. He treats those topics in LJ, but not as extensively as polygamy (on consanguineous marriage and incest, see especially 163–68, 441, 446–48).

In *The Theory of Moral Sentiments*, in speaking of sympathy and concern among family members, Smith gives two paragraphs to a contrast between "pastoral countries" and "commercial countries," relating familial sentiments to "the authority of law" and, implicitly, to kin structure. "In commercial countries, where the authority of law is always perfectly sufficient to protect the meanest man in the state, the descendants of the same family, having no such motive for keeping together, naturally separate and disperse, as interest or inclination may direct" (TMS 223.13).

Smith makes a similar connection between commerce, kin-networks, and development in *Wealth of Nations*, Book III: Of the different Progress of Opulence in different Nations. Chapter IV is about how the towns contribute to the improvement to the countryside. As the commercial towns grow in size and power, and the country begins to improve, the kin-networks of the barons are slowly eroded. The kin-networks based on blood, marriage, and honor are replaced with social networks based on commercial ties. Barons become gentlemen. Without the kin-networks, and with gentlemen able to split inheritance among their children, the successive wealth of each generation decreases. Smith notes that "in commercial countries, therefore, riches, in spite of the most violent regulations of law to prevent their dissipation, very seldom remain long in the same family" (WN 422). Families meet not on violent terms, but on civil and economic ones instead. The polity can focus on improving the polity, rather than fighting.

References

Henrich, Joseph, Robert Boyd, and Peter J. Richerson. 2012. The Puzzle of Monogamous Marriage. *Philosophical Transactions of the Royal Society* 367(1589): 657–669.

Henrich, Joseph. 2016. *The Secret of Our Success: How Culture Is Driving Human Evolution, Domesticating Our Species, and Making Us Smarter.* Princeton; Oxford: Princeton University Press.

Hume, David. 1985. *Essays: Moral, Political and Literary,* ed. Eugene F. Miller. Indianapolis: Liberty Fund.

North, Douglass C., John Joseph Wallis, and Barry R. Weingast. 2009. *Violence and Social Orders: A Conceptual Framework for Interpreting Recorded Human History.* Cambridge: Cambridge University Press.

Schulz, Jonathan F. 2022. Kin Networks and Institutional Development. *The Economic Journal* 132(647): 2578-2613.

Smith, Adam. 1982 [1776]. *An Inquiry into the Nature and Causes of the Wealth of Nations,* eds. R.H. Campbell and A.S. Skinner. 2 vols. Indianapolis: Liberty Fund.

Smith, Adam. 1982 [1759]. *The Theory of Moral Sentiments,* eds. D.D. Raphael and A.L. Macfie. Indianapolis: Liberty Fund.

Smith, Adam. 1982. *Lectures on Jurisprudence,* eds. R. L. Meek, D. D. Raphael, and P. G. Stein. Indianapolis: Liberty Fund.

CHAPTER 11

Signaling Smith's System through "By the Same Author"

Caroline Breashears

P aratexts are materials on the borders of the text, such as the title page, epigraph, table of contents, and index. The kind of paratext that concerns us here is the "by the same author" list. We find something interesting about "by the same author" in the early editions of Adam Smith's *Wealth of Nations*. I show images from the first and second edition and address how they were intended to shape their interpretations of Smith's works as a whole. This article is a riff on an article in *Economic Affairs* by Dan Klein and me.

Gérard Genette suggests that paratexts offer a "threshold" designed to ensure "a better reception for the text and a more pertinent reading of it" (1997, 2). While the list of works "by the same author" was a common paratext in Smith's time, the placement in early editions of *Wealth of Nations* was unusual and goes beyond advertising Smith's earlier publications. Specifically, in the editions published in 1776 and 1778, the author-works lists reinforce Smith's overarching system across *The Theory of Moral Sentiments*, the essay on languages, and *Wealth of Nations*.

"Published by the same AUTHOR"

As Genette observes, "the list of works 'By the same author' [was] generally placed at the beginning of the volume (facing the title page) or at the end" (1997, 99). In 1776, however, William Strahan and Thomas Cadell published the first edition of *Wealth of Nations* with the author-works list directly opposite the table of contents (Figure 1).

FIGURE 1: *WEALTH OF* NATIONS (1776)

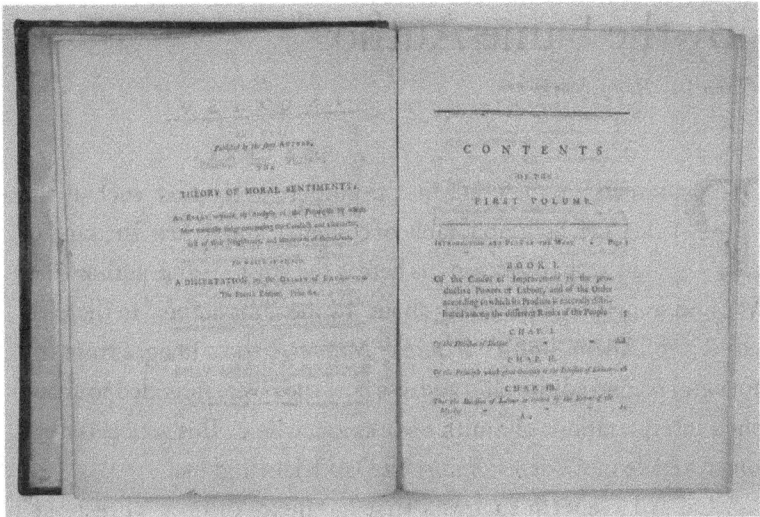

Image courtesy of St. Lawrence University Library

This placement was uncommon, as shown by a methodical search in the database *Eighteenth-Century Collections Online* (ECCO) focused on books published between 1759 and 1790 by "Strahan or Cadell" and including the phrase "by the same author." Our search returned 160 books, all of which included an author-works list or a variation on it. The author-works list appears most commonly at the end of the book (91 of 160), and often before or on the title page (23 of the 160). Only three books, including Smith's *Wealth of Nations* (1776), placed the author-works list directly opposite the table of contents. In these three instances, that list functions as an advertisement, but its placement also prepares readers to see connections between the author's previous works and the new text.

The placement of Smith's author-works list signals that *Wealth of Nations* continues a system. As Figure 1 shows, Strahan and Cadell give the full titles of both *The Theory of Moral Sentiments* and its appendix, *A Dissertation on the Origin of Language*. This list of works "Published by the same Author" establishes Smith's expertise and invites readers to see *Wealth of Nations* (WN) as ongoing elaboration of a unified body of thought. WN enlarges the Smithian outlook.

In *The Enlightenment and the Book* (2006), Richard Sher writes that for Scottish authors, the "union of text and paratext was crucial for their personal reputations as authors" (p. 194). Sher emphasizes the importance of "the coherence and authenticity of the public's image of the author as an individual whose works were joined together to form a unified and immediately recognizable whole" (pp. 159-160). Ian Ross (2010, p. 286) also notes the placement, observing that Smith or his publisher wanted readers to remember he was the author of *The Theory of Moral Sentiments*. These goals—advertising Smith's previous book and suggesting connections between the preceding works and the current one—extended to the second edition of *Wealth of Nations*.

In the 1778 edition, the placement of the author-works list moves to *after* the table of contents and opposite the start of Smith's "Introduction and Plan of the Work," as shown in Figure 2.

FIGURE 2: PARATEXT FROM *THE WEALTH OF NATIONS* (1778)

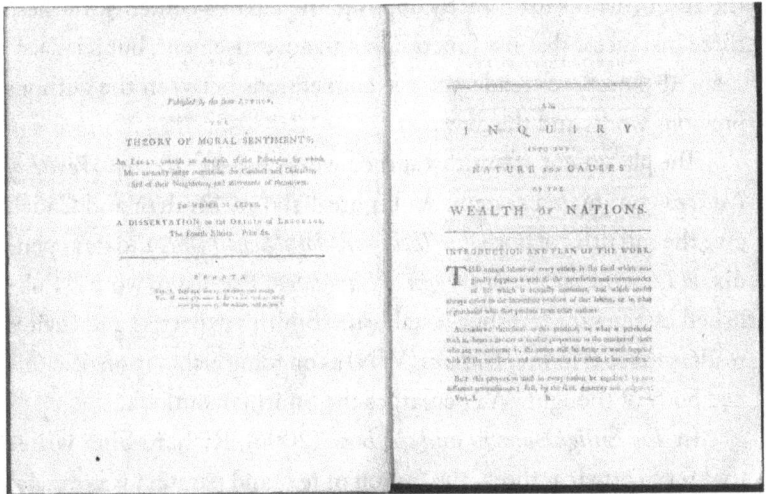

Image courtesy of Special Collections Research Center, William & Mary Libraries

The placement in 1778 is more common than that of 1776: our search identified 23 other examples. These publications are, however, restricted to relatively few authors. In all examples, the list of the author's previous publications establishes his expertise and an argumentative thread across books. The author-works list serves a similar purpose in Smith's *Wealth of Nations* (1778), highlighting his interest in the principles of judgment (TMS) and the springs of exchange (the Language essay) emphasized in the Introduction to WN.

Searching personal correspondence, we find no evidence that Smith or his publishers intended for readers to see these particular connections. Also, they did not sustain this unusual placement of "by the same author" in the other editions of WN published during

Smith's lifetime.[1] Yet if Smith's goals were to draw readers to his latest book and emphasize its connection to TMS, then he and his publishers may have felt they had already succeeded in signaling the unity of Smith's works.

Connecting Smith's writings

Modern editions of Smith's works have eliminated the "by the same author" list. That is unfortunate, because that paratext in the first two editions of WN suggests philosophical connections across three texts:

1. The Language essay
2. The full title of *The Theory of Moral Sentiments* (TMS)
3. WN under the ethical umbrella of TMS.[2]

In reading Smith's writings, our understanding of a part informs our understanding of the whole, while our understanding of the whole informs that of each part. The early WN "by the same author" lists helped us see how the parts complement one another and form a profound whole.

Smith's Language essay first appeared in 1761 in *The Philological Miscellany*. The full title is "Considerations concerning the first formation of Languages, and the different genius of original and com-

---

1. Smith spent much of the years 1773 to 1777 in London, enabling in-person communication with his publishers and printers. We have zero correspondence to or from Strahan or Cadell from 1767 until after WN was published in 1776. We know nothing of Smith's instructions for WN's printing and paratext in 1776 and 1778.

2. As Erik Matson (2022, 269-273) puts it, there are two major problems in the Glasgow edition of the TMS volume. Both concern elements shown in Figure 1. One is the severing of the Language essay. The other is the failure to provide the full title of TMS on the title-page of the TMS volume—only in passing do the editors D.D. Raphael and A.L. Macfie provide the full title, on page 40 of their introduction. Raphael and Macfie do not explain why they made these changes.

pounded Languages," which appeared on the title page and in the table of contents from the third edition of TMS (1767) and thereafter. The Language essay has extensive connections to both TMS and WN. For instance, the appending of the Language essay to TMS helps to make explicit deeper-evolution ideas that had been only implicit in TMS. In the Language essay, Smith writes: "The general rule would establish itself insensibly, and by slow degrees" (211). Such development parallels the spontaneous generation of proprieties in TMS. Indeed, language norms live in discourse, and discourse is a form of conduct, so language norms *are* proprieties. In discoursing, one's semantics and syntax can be praiseworthy or blameworthy, virtuous or vicious.

Seeing the title of the Language essay opposite the table of contents of WN (1776) also reinforces Smith's understanding of connections across disciplines. Language not only develops "insensibly." It is also, Smith hints, fundamental to trade. In WN, he refuses to name explicitly the origin of our "propensity to truck, barter, and exchange," but he does suggest that it "seems more probable, it be the necessary consequence of the faculties of reason and speech" (25.2). Likewise, it is crucial to read *Wealth of Nations* in relation to *The Theory of Moral Sentiments*. TMS is about seeing beauty and deformity in human conduct, or judging human conduct. WN instructs us in properly judging the conduct of those who make government policy, those who pursue honest income, and those who pursue dishonest income through government-conferred privilege.

Smith prepared readers for the content of *Wealth of Nations* at the end of early editions of *The Theory of Moral Sentiments*, where he looks forward to expounding on "the general principles which ought to run through and be the foundation of the laws of nations" (341.37). In his final edition of TMS (1790), Smith returns to this promise in another piece of paratext, his Advertisement. In so doing, Smith reinforces his sense of his own *oeuvre*:

In the last paragraph of the first Edition of the present work, I said, that I should in another discourse endeavour to give an account of the general principles of law and government, and of the different revolutions which they had undergone in the different ages and periods of society; not only in what concerns justice, but in what concerns police, revenue, and arms, and whatever else is the object of law. In the *Enquiry concerning the Nature and Causes of the Wealth of Nations*, I have partly executed this promise; at least so far as concerns police, revenue, and arms. What remains, the theory of jurisprudence, which I have long projected, I have hitherto been hindered from executing, by the same occupations which had till now prevented me from revising the present work. (3)

The placement and the argument of this paratext reinforce our point about the significance of the paratextual materials in WN.

Don't expect too much from civilization

The final words of the Language essay say that Latin's conciseness, versification, and sweetness made perfection of beauty much more acquirable "than it can be to those whose expression is constantly confined by the prolixness, constraint, and monotony of modern languages" (226). These final words strike a dour note. Since the essay is an appendix which concludes TMS, that work itself ends on that dour note. This final phrase – "confined by the prolixness, constraint, and monotony of modern languages" – brings to mind the final words of WN, that Great Britain should "endeavour to accommodate her future views and designs to the real mediocrity of her circumstances" (WN, 947.92). Thus, Smith does not conclude with a zeal for progress. There is no promise of an integral, poetic life. In the Language essay, Smith explains, "mankind have learned by degrees to *split* and *divide* almost every event into a great number of metaphysical parts, expressed by the different parts of speech, variously combined in the different members of every phrase and sentence" (1983, p. 217; emphasis added). Dividing and subdividing is a main theme in WN. It is a central point of the Language essay, and we may read it into the rest of TMS. With the Language essay appended to TMS, both of Smith's two great works end on a dour note.

Smith tended to presuppose that his readers enjoy stable, functional government. He counsels us to reform policy, if only gradually, in the direction of "the liberal plan" (WN 664.3), for the alternatives are worse. The unity of Smith's thought tends toward the prospect of peaceful enjoyment of our circumstances with a sober regard for neighbors. Even if one's small life within the modern liberal commercial society feels monotonous, Smith's conception of the common good in the modern world is not without its lustre. Seeing Smith's paratextual materials, we recover some of the fullness of Smith's outlook for human life in modern times.

References

Berry, Christopher J. 1974. Adam Smith's Considerations on Language. *Journal of the History of Ideas* 35(1): 130-138.

Genette, Gerard. 1997. *Paratexts: Thresholds of Interpretation (Literature, Culture, Theory, Series Number 20)*, trans. Jane E. Lewin. Cambridge: Cambridge University Press.

Klein, Daniel B., and Caroline Breashears. 2022. By the Same Author: Presenting Adam Smith's Works as a Whole. *Economic Affairs* 42(3): 528-540.

Matson, Erik W. 2022. God, Commerce, and Adam Smith through the Editions of *The Theory of Moral Sentiments*. *Journal of Markets & Morality* 24(2): 269-288.

Ross, Ian Simpson. 2010. *The Life of Adam Smith*. Second edition. Oxford: Oxford University Press.

Sher, Richard B. 2006. *The Enlightenment and the Book: Scottish Authors and Their Pub-*

lishers in Eighteenth-Century Britain, Ireland, and America. University of Chicago Press.

Smith, Adam. 1976 [1776]. *An Inquiry into the Nature and Causes of the Wealth of Nations,* eds. R.H. Campbell and A.S. Skinner. Oxford: Oxford University Press. Indianapolis: Liberty Fund, 1981.

Smith, Adam. 1790. *The Theory of Moral Sentiments,* eds. D.D. Raphael and A.L. Macfie. Oxford: Oxford University Press, 1976.

Smith, Adam. 1977 (Corr.). *The Correspondence of Adam Smith,* eds. Ernest C. Mossner and Ian Simpson Ross. Oxford: Clarendon Press.

Smith, Adam. 1983 (LRBL). *Lectures on Rhetoric and Belles Lettres,* ed. J. C. Bryce. Oxford: Clarendon Press.

CHAPTER 12

Adam Smith on the Rich and the Poor

Christopher Martin

Adam Smith has often been seen as a defender of one's own and therefore of the rich. Because of this emphasis on one's own, he has sometimes been represented as cool towards working people or the poor. However, scholars have offered other views of Smith. Some go so far as to view him as a kind of proto-progressive (Fleischacker 2004, Rothschild 1992).

Was Smith's attitude toward the poor a chilly one? In 1891, the great Austrian economist (and admirer of Smith) Carl Menger said otherwise:

> In every conflict of interest between the rich and the poor, the strong and the weak, Smith sides without exception with the latter. I use the term "without exception" with proper consideration, as one cannot find one single instance in the works of Smith in which he represents the interests of the rich and powerful against the poor and weak. (Menger 2016, 475)

I too am an admirer of Adam Smith. When I first encountered

Menger's claim, I thrilled to it. At the same time, however, I felt skeptical. *The Wealth of Nations* (WN) alone is a huge work, to say nothing of Smith's writings discovered after Menger published these words in 1891. Could Menger's strong claim survive careful scrutiny?

I wondered about the "without exception." As the survivor of a ponderous but (I think) conscientious scholarly effort (Martin 2021), I actually can offer a "fact-checking" report on it of sorts. To the question "did Adam Smith indeed always side with the poor and weak against the rich and powerful" I give the resounding answer: *Yes, mostly. It's a little complicated*. Fact-checking isn't always as easy as we hope!

In many cases Smith *does* clearly advocate for the interests and welfare of the poor, of workers, of the politically powerless, and so forth. But at times Smith's discussion is harder to characterize. It turns out that, to echo Menger's words, what "siding with" or "representing the interests of" some group in society means depends on what policies one thinks are in the best interest of the group. To use a perennial contemporary policy dispute as an example, whether opposition to minimum wage laws is "anti-worker" depends on what the disemployment and other adverse effects of such policies actually are, which is a complex matter (Reich et.al. 2017; Jardim et.al. 2022). Smith tackled similarly knotty issues—what are the effects of free markets on the welfare of the poor? Of the division of labor? Of various sorts of taxes? Of different means of financing education and religious instruction?

Adam Smith, hot and cold

By quoting selectively from the WN and the *Lectures on Jurisprudence* (LJ), it is possible to paint two diametrically opposed pictures of Adam Smith. The "warm" Smith makes statements that could come from a beret-wearing radical. The "cool" Smith can sound like a Dickensian villain.

The "warm" Adam Smith dwells on the prima facie unfairness of life in an advanced economy with specialization and wage labor. He notes that "[t]he division of opulence [wealth] is not according to the work": a rich merchant works less but earns more than his clerk; the clerk, in turn, earns more and enjoys better working conditions than the manual laborer who "trudges up and down without intermission." Indeed, "[He] who…bears the burthen of society has the fewest advantages" (LJ, 489-490). In an earlier version of this same point Smith used even more emotional language, describing the "dependent poor man" who

> …furnishes the means of the convenience and ease of all the rest [of society]…[but] is himself possessed of a very small share and is buried in obscurity. He bears on his shoulders the whole of mankind, and unable to sustain the load is buried by the weight of it and thrust down into the lowest parts of the earth, from whence he supports all the rest. (LJ, 341)

Elsewhere, Smith claims that the rich gain proportionately more from trade (with the poor) than the poor do (LJ, 512); that "[l]aws and government may be considered in this and indeed in every case as a combination of the rich to oppress the poor, and preserve to themselves…inequality" (LJ, 208). He describes the contemporary "poor day labourer or indigent farmer" as being subject to "oppression and tyranny" (LJ, 338-339). Seeming to foreshadow contemporary debates, Smith further says that "[w]herever there is great property, there is great inequality" and explicitly claims that "[f]or one very rich man, there must be at least five hundred poor, and the affluence of the few supposes the indigence of the many" (WN, 709-710).

Yet, a "cool" version of Adam Smith can also be selectively constructed. This Smith describes the poor as making "inroads" and "attacks'" on the rich which can only be repelled by the outstretched "arm of authority" (LJ, 208). Civil government is needed to protect owners against the "violence and rapacity" of the poor and to thereby preserve the "usefull inequality in the fortunes of mankind" (LJ, 338; Martin 2021, 842). In the *Theory of Moral Sentiments* (TMS) Smith argues that the "poor man must neither defraud nor steal from the rich" even if the gain from such a transaction were "much more beneficial [to the poor man] than the loss could be hurtful to the [rich]" (TMS, 138). In *LJ*, he even criticizes the intelligence of the poor, saying that "the low people are exceedingly stupid" due in part to parents neglecting to educate their children. Such children when grown have no recreation except riot and debauchery, so they work half the week and carouse the second half (LJ, 540). In the WN (795), Smith says that many of the urban poor abandon themselves "to every sort of low profligacy and vice." The fact that "the people who cloath the whole world are in rags themselves" is seemingly partly their own fault (LJ, 539-540). Now we seem very far from Smith the radical partisan of the workers!

An underlying unity

Of course, each of these portrayals misses the underlying unity of Smith's thought. He had both a strong and even impassioned sympathy for the poor and a strong commitment to property, with the second commitment justified partly by the first. In many of the passages quoted above, Smith dwells so long on the disadvantages of being a worker in an advanced economy in order to highlight just how compelling the advantages are. The famous culmination of this strategy is Smith's claim, appearing in similar phrasing in both the LJ and in the *Wealth of Nations*, that even a common day laborer in Britain is more equipped with the "conveniencies and luxuries of life" than an "Indian prince" with 1,000 subjects (LJ, 338-339; WN version at 22-24). The resolution of the apparent paradox is the enormous increase in productivity conferred by the division of labor. Even the "meanest laborer in a polished society" can focus on a specific task and become good at it; he is also assisted in his work by "machines and instruments" that primitive man lacks (LJ, 521). The things he buys only appear simple; even the common woolen coat he wears is itself a masterpiece of coordination (WN, 22-23). But the division of labor requires that property be secure. If not, if

> people find themselves every moment in danger of being robbed of all they possess, they have no motive to be industrious. There could be little accumulation of stock, because the indolent...would live upon the industrious, and spend whatever they produced. (LJ, 521)

The mention of "stock" (capital) is significant. Capital is essential both for purchasing machinery and tools and to finance the complex organizations and trading patterns supporting the division of labor itself. Its creation requires strong property rights, for otherwise it is under threat from the "passion to invade property" which comes from "avarice and ambition in the rich, in the poor the hatred of labour and the love of present ease and enjoyment" (WN, 709). Notice that property can come under threat from *both* the poor and the rich.

That Smith is an "equal opportunity defender" of property is further suggested by his discussion of poverty in China (WN, 112). Smith contends that there "the rich or the owners of large capitals enjoy a great deal of security." Were Smith an advocate only for the interests of the rich he would have stopped there. But he continues that "the poor or the owners of small capitals enjoy scarce any [security], but are liable, under the pretence of justice, to be pillaged and plundered at any time by the inferior mandarins." As a result, he concludes, less capital is accumulated than China could in fact sustain (see discussion at Martin 2021, 845). This passage supports two complementary interpretations. First, that it is *unjust* to pillage the poor. Second, that it is *bad for economic growth* to pillage them. Put another way, economic development isn't a "trickle-down" process from the rich but a broad-based process in which all can participate—the proverbial rising tide that raises all boats, a theme set out in the fourth paragraph of WN (10).

Everyone's wellbeing counts when evaluating the growth process. Against the early modern tradition that the prosperity of the working class somehow didn't sum towards national well-being, Smith contended that "[n]o society can surely be flourishing and happy, of which the far greater part of the members are poor and miserable." Moreover, it was only "equity, besides, that they who feed, cloath, and lodge the whole body of the people, should....be themselves tolerably well fed, cloathed, and lodged" (WN, 95-96).

While the second part of this statement has been taken by some to suggest endorsement of some kind of government-organized redistribution, it can be argued that what Smith intended was rather the removal of restrictions on workers' ability to gain wealth through market transactions. Of these there were still many in the eighteenth century; the apprenticeship system for one, and for another a crumbling, imperfectly enforced, but still threatening legal apparatus to confine the poor within their home parishes—and its limited labor market (discussed in Martin 2015). Smith treated these policies as property issues, liberty issues. His anger is palpable when he asserts

> The property which every man has in his own labour...is
> the most sacred and inviolable. The patrimony of a poor
> man lies in the strength and dexterity of his hands; and to

hinder him from employing this strength and dexterity…
without injury to his neighbour, is a plain violation of this
most sacred property…a manifest encroachment upon the
just liberty both of the workman, and of those who might
be disposed to employ him. (WN, 138)

Likewise, the labor mobility restriction (the Law of Settlement)
wasn't just an "inefficiency" or policy error, but an "evident violation
of natural liberty and justice" (WN, 157). Smith never, to my knowledge, talks about injustice to the rich with the same warmth as he
does injustice to the poor. And therein may glimmer another facet
of his thought.

Smith has a reputation for caginess and hedging his statements
(Henderson 2004). It might therefore be justifiable (if, admittedly, a
bit speculative) to scrutinize his statements about rich-poor conflicts
based on the type of rich person in question. It is plausible that the
rich who Smith criticizes obtained their wealth through zero-sum or
even negative-sum processes. The rich often wield centralized political power abusively, such as the employers who ask Parliament to limit
the wage of journeymen tailors (WN, 157–158) or the wealthy master
manufacturers who orchestrate and benefit from the mercantile system (WN, 644). In a society rife with special legal privileges, Smith
may well have suspected that someone rich would also be powerful.
Being powerful in turn often spelled involvement in predatory avarice—even though wealth gained fairly was not in itself objectionable
(TMS, 83; Martin 2021, 843).

What I'm trying to suggest is that we cannot summarize Smith's
attitudes with some bland statement that "there is no ultimate conflict
of interest between rich and poor." Whether there is a conflict depends
on what sort of rich people we are talking about. It also depends on
the type of society in which both rich and poor are embedded. Smith

makes clear his belief that the poor are better off in an advanced market order enjoying an approximation to the "liberal plan of equality, liberty, and justice" (WN, 664) rather than living under feudalism or in the slaveholding economy of the ancient world.

And Smith argued that with liberty comes dignity. Smith says that dependency (i.e., being a retainer or servant) "corrupt[s] and enervate[s] and debase[s] the mind" but that commerce and manufacturing prevents this degradation by giving the poor alternative and better job opportunities than working for the rich. Commercial society even gives the independent common people of England "noble and generous notions of probity" (LJ, 1762–63, vi.4-7, 332; LJ, 1766, 204-205, 486-7). Unlike the shepherds of the remote past who had to serve their local aristocrat (LJ, 202), a tradesman in a commercial society with many customers isn't beholden to any one individual, even a wealthy one. It is perhaps notable that the laborer who was thrust into the "depths of the earth" is described by Smith as a "*dependent* poor man" (LJ, 341, emphasis added). That market society reduces "servile dependency," promoting instead "independency" (412, 399), is a main theme of Book III of the WN (412, 399).

Compared to what?

Of course, manufacturing and commerce can also fall prey to exploitive behavior. Government mercantilist restrictions encourage "industry which is carried on for the benefit of the rich and the powerful," while "[t]hat which is carried on for the benefit of the poor and the indigent [for example, spinning woolen yarn] is too often either neglected or oppressed" (WN, 644). Even in the Britain of his day, Smith says, some of the wealthy act to the detriment of the good of the common people.

Adam Smith's "relevance" for modern debates around wealth and poverty has obvious limitations. Smith's belief that the standard of living was rising in Britain in the 18th century isn't particularly useful for contemporary arguments about the recent trajectory of real wages. Paradoxically, then, his "bigger picture" frameworks—those less dependent on specific details of his own time—tend to be most provocative for his remote intellectual descendants. His observation that a poor person might simultaneously have a "very small share" of the total wealth of society, but a "great share" of the "conveniencies of life," obviously anticipates the distinction between absolute and relative poverty (LJ, 341 as well as similar comments at 338-339 and in WN, 22-24). A modern reader is naturally led to wonder whether well-being scales in exactly this way, or if there are certain goods whose accessibility depends on relative and not just absolute earnings. Weighing these issues alongside Smith's claim that "[i]n what constitutes the real happiness of human life...all the different ranks of life are nearly upon a level" (TMS, 185) opens rich directions for thought.

Smith was suspicious of sweeping changes imposed by arrogant reformers. He still had an "idea of the perfection of policy" and wished to see the status quo improved even if he knew that his ideas would, realistically, never triumph completely (TMS, 234; WN, 471, 616–617). But even the best policy regime would not deliver paradise. There is no reason to suppose that each and every element of liberal commercial society contributes to human wellbeing. Far from it. But decisions in life always come to the question, Compared to what? And Smith thought that the liberal plan was better than the alternatives. If we too struggle to bridge the gap between the status quo and "perfect justice...perfect liberty...[and] perfect equality" (WN, 669), we can at least feel that Smith would sympathize with our efforts.

References

Fleischacker, Samuel. 2004. *On Adam Smith's Wealth of Nations*. Princeton: Princeton University Press.

Henderson, Willie. 2004. A Very Cautious, or a Very Polite, Dr Smith? Hedging in the Wealth of Nations. In *The Adam Smith Review: Volume 1*, ed. Vivienne Brown, 72–96. London: Routledge.

Jardim, Ekaterina, Mark C. Long, Robert Plotnick, Emma Van Inwegen, Jacob Vigdor, and Hilary Wething. 2022. Minimum-wage Increases and Low-wage Employment: Evidence from Seattle. *American Economic Journal: Economic Policy* 14(2): 263-314.

Martin, Christopher S. 2015. Equity, Besides: Adam Smith and the Utility of Poverty. *Journal of the History of Economic Thought* 37(4): 559–81.

Martin, Christopher. 2021. Adam Smith and the Poor: A Textual Analysis. *Journal of Economic Behavior & Organization* 184: 837–49.

Menger, Carl. 2016. The Social Theories of Classical Political Economy and Modern Economic Policy. Translated by Stefan Kolev and Erwin Dekker. *Econ Journal Watch* 13(3): 467–89.

Reich, Michael, Sylvia Allegretto, and Anna Godøy. 2017. Seattle's Minimum Wage Experience 2015-16. *CWED Policy Brief*. Berkeley, CA: Center on Wage and Employment Dynamics.

Rothschild, Emma. 1992. Adam Smith and Conservative Economics. *The Economic History Review*, New Series, 45(1): 74–96.

Smith, Adam. 1981. *An Inquiry into the Nature and Causes of the Wealth of Nations*, eds. R.H. Campbell, A.S. Skinner, and W.B Todd. Indianapolis, IN: Liberty Fund.

Smith, Adam. 1982. *The Theory of Moral Sentiments*, eds. D.D. Raphael and A.L. Macfie. Indianapolis, IN: Liberty Fund.

Smith, Adam. 2009. *Lectures on Jurisprudence*, eds. R. L. Meek, D. D. Raphael, and P. G. Stein. Indianapolis, IN: Liberty Fund.

CHAPTER 13

Moral Judgment and Governmentalizing Social Affairs

Paul D. Mueller

Adam Smith advocated free markets and limited government. He wrote extensively about the mistakes, abuses, and distorted incentives created by certain government interventions. He also made a case for limited government—especially at the national level—through reflections on the nature of human judgment. He argued that as we move from concrete, private contexts to more general and abstract contexts, there is a natural rise in the hazard of the corruption of judgment. Both the intentions and the effects of government quickly become abstract. As our ideas become more abstract, however, our moral judgment can more easily be skewed, warped, or corrupted. This has significant implications for what can sometimes be a fine line between good governance and harmful regulation and over-governance—"governmentalization."

Smith was no anarchist or revolutionary. He believed firmly in the rule of law and the value of established political authority. Yet, as he elaborates throughout the *Wealth of Nations*, a good many government policies are harmful. In this essay I show how the ideas Smith developed in *The Theory of Moral Sentiments* further undergird his arguments for limited and local government. Leaving social affairs voluntary and governance local helps keep our moral judgment on a healthy footing. We should resist governmentalizing social affairs, prudently roll back existing governmentalization, and promote a robust principle of voluntary association.

Real vs. imagined utility

Smith's argument against governmentalizing social affairs builds on moral psychology. The moral corruption that grows in highly governmentalized social affairs has both epistemological and psychological sources. To address the matter, I turn to a part in *The Theory of Moral Sentiments* (TMS) in which Smith develops his idea about how we rely on fittingness or propriety in making decisions, rather than a calculus of the consequences—partly because making such a calculus is often impossible.

In Part IV, Ch. 1 of TMS, Smith develops the relationship between the imagined and the actual utility of objects, choices, and policies in three parallel contexts: trinkets, private life, and public life. "Utility" means beneficialness, both to the whole society and to the individual acting. Smith focuses on how the concreteness versus abstractness affects the imagined utility to the individual or to society. As Smith addresses actual and imagined utility in the three contexts—trinkets, private life, and public life—he moves from the more concrete to the more abstract. And he suggests that with that movement people's moral judgments worsen. Smith describes how a sense of fitness or aptness of an object for serving some useful function often means more to us than its actual usefulness:

> But that this fitness, this happy contrivance of any production of art, should often be more valued, than the very end

for which it was intended; and that *the exact adjustment of the means for attaining any conveniency or pleasure, should frequently be more regarded, than that very conveniency or pleasure, in the attainment of which their whole merit would seem to consist*, has not, so far as I know, been taken notice of by any body. (TMS 179-180; emphasis added)

While it seems that we should value objects or choices based upon how much utility they bring us, quite often we value them based on how well we think they *are suited* to bring us utility, whether or not they really do.

Smith then gives many contexts in which the "fitness" sensibility operates: "That this however is very frequently the case, may be observed in a thousand instances, both in *the most frivolous and in the most important concerns of human life*" (TMS 180, emphasis added).

Trinkets

Smith begins with "trinkets." He claims that many people would feel dissatisfied with a watch that lost a minute of time every week. Some might even sell such a watch and spend a significant sum of money buying one that doesn't lose any time. But why? The old watch served quite well enough to give us a good sense for when we ought to be somewhere. And, as Smith observes, people who buy the new watch:

> will not always be found either more scrupulously punctual than other men, or more anxiously concerned upon any other account, to know precisely what time of day it is. What interests him is not so much the attainment of this piece of knowledge, as the perfection of the machine which serves to attain it. (TMS 180)

Smith also highlights the impulse of a man whose housekeeper will tomorrow straighten a disorderly room he enters. The mess may not inhibit the man's present course of action in the slightest. And yet, Smith says, a man disturbed by the departure from the accustomed and fitting order:

> voluntarily puts himself to more trouble than all he could have suffered from the want of it; since nothing was more easy, than to have set himself down upon one of [the chairs], which is probably what he does when his labour is over. What he wanted therefore, it seems, was not so much this conveniency, as that arrangement of things which promotes it. (TMS 180)

As the father of five young children, constantly battling with chaos, I can attest that Smith is on to something here!

We like things to be orderly and well-suited towards some end, even if we do not ultimately achieve that end ourselves. In matters of the watch or organizing a room, this curious divide between imagined utility and actual utility may not be all that significant. But when it comes to how we order our personal lives, this divide can be the source of trouble and difficulty. And when it comes to public life, it can be the source of disaster and ruin.

Private life

In the same chapter of TMS Part IV, we find the parable of the poor man's son. The son "admires the condition of the rich" and becomes captivated by the *imagined* ease and tranquility he will have with riches—a commodious house, easy travel, good food, and so on. He pursues his ambition even though becoming rich is difficult: "to obtain the conveniences which these afford, he submits in the first year, nay in the first month of his application, to more fatigue of body and more uneasiness of mind than he could have suffered through the whole of his life from the want of them" (TMS 181). Still, his imagination and the desired utility of wealth spur him on.

Yet, toward the end of his life, he makes another discovery, namely that "wealth and greatness are mere trinkets of frivolous utility, no more suited" to promoting ease and utility than the literal trinkets of watches and tweezer cases that we value for their imagined utility. The son's imagination of the utility of wealth does not match reality.

Smith even calls this incongruence "a deception"—but a useful one, if only from a social point of view. For this deception leads the poor man's son to industry and to serve his fellow man. It is in this chapter that the sole mention of the invisible hand in TMS occurs, leading those who pursue or who have wealth to benefit the poor unwittingly:

> They are led by an invisible hand to make nearly the same distribution of the necessaries of life, which would have been made, had the earth been divided into equal portions among all its inhabitants, and thus without intending it, without knowing it, advance the interest of society, and afford means of the multiplication of the species. (TMS 184-185)

Although one might pity the poor man's son, his self-deception is his own and his industriousness renders benefits to others.

In trinkets and baubles, the connections between the intended utility, the object, and the actual utility are fairly clear and observable. As for the objects of private life, much more time and perspective are required to accurately assess how one's actions, imagined utility, and actual utility are connected, or not. There is greater abstraction involved when assessing the suitability of one's chosen profession and the imagined utility one seeks to achieve. Still, it is the same person choosing, imagining, experiencing, and reflecting.

Public life—and the pitfalls of governmentalization

Smith does not take an "invisible hand" view of the divide between imagined utility and actual utility when it comes to public life. Coercion and force are the tools of public life, rather than voluntary exchange. With only weak correction mechanisms in public life, the abstractness of what one proposes leads to ongoing distortion of one's moral judgment.

Smith writes that we imagine how an impartial spectator would judge our decisions. To do this well, we often require feedback and the assistance or experience of actual spectators. Rubbing shoulders with our peers and equals helps us to understand both impartiality and the idea of spectators judging our actions. Factions are a source of corruption in both private and public life. When we are part of a faction, our peers and "spectators" have built-in partiality. Yet we come to view their partiality as impartial because it seems universally held within our circle of peers.

Consider the example of political parties. What seems reasonable or appropriate in a political rally often varies drastically from what we find appropriate in other contexts. Similarly, national conflicts promote partiality. Smith argues that people living in one country in conflict with another have a difficult time forming impartial judgments about the conflict—they are immersed in a society of "partial" spectators who share similar perspectives on the matter.

Politicians and bureaucrats also face the problem of living in an echo chamber. They are surrounded by people who are not likely to be impartial: their staff, lobbyists, and the fellow partisans of their party. As a result, they are less likely to see themselves as being "but one of the multitude, in no respect better than any other in it" (TMS 137). And this means that as they consider the virtue of their choices and actions, their judgments are more likely skewed or partial than those of ordinary citizens who rub shoulders with their equals every day. The partiality of peers corrupts moral judgment—and this problem is more prevalent in political settings.

But a second hazard more prevalent in political decision-making is the lack of direct feedback of the effects of one's decisions. When a politician proposes some course of legislative action, the imagined utility is necessarily abstract, as it will affect many people in varied ways. What's more, the actual utility of such policies may be impossible to discern because it is experienced by people in ways that defy aggregation—very much like the Hayekian knowledge problem faced by central planners. So how is a politician, or his myriad followers, or voters in general, to know whether the actual utility of his plan lives up to the imagined utility? Smith suggests that often he can't, at least not in any direct, immediate fashion. The direct effects of national laws, for example, are difficult to decipher and often create unintended and overlooked consequences.

And here lies a major problem with political centralization and governmentalizing social affairs. The feedback of actual usefulness and the feedback of (supposedly impartial) spectators are lacking or faulty. How is the representative from Bath or Birmingham to consider sanitation policy in London judiciously? It is in light of such difficulties in judgment that Smith offers the "liberal plan" for government and society. His plan, in the main, is to relieve the government of many assumed obligations:

> Every man, as long as he does not violate the laws of justice, is left perfectly free to pursue his own interest his

own way... The sovereign is completely discharged from a duty, in the attempting to perform which *he must always be exposed to innumerable delusions*, and for the proper performance of which no human wisdom or knowledge could ever be sufficient; the duty of superintending the industry of private people... (WN 687, emphasis added)

Although Smith acknowledges the role of government as a "nightwatchman" along with a potential role providing basic public-goods, the presumption weighs against governmentalizing social affairs. Even with governmental provision of public goods like street lamps, canals, or roads, Smith says local provision is far superior to national provision; and funding should be provided principally by user fees. That makes the policy more concrete and less abstract with more real as opposed to imagined feedback, and more easily observed utility.

The concern of governmentalization tending towards moral corruption also relates to Smith's arguments that workers and employers should be free to arrange labor contracts how they see fit; that tariffs and subsidies should generally be avoided; and that the owners of capital should be free to decide what to do with it. These individuals nearly always have the healthiest feedback mechanisms, the best incentives, and the best knowledge to make decisions.

Where social affairs are free from governmentalization, people operate in contexts that promote more robust moral judgments. People better find the path of virtue. And that, too, can be incorporated into our thinking about beneficialness or social utility. Smith cares not only about having a prosperous society, he wants a moral and virtuous society too.

CHAPTER 14

Adam Smith and the Labor Theory of Value

John A. Robinson and J. Robert Subrick

It is said that Adam Smith advanced something called "the labor theory of value" but what does that mean?

Let's say the product is a pin. And let's say it is produced in a pin factory owned by Pippin, who employs workers.

Taking explanation as the backbone of theory, let's break the "labor theory of value" down:

- What is being explained?

- What is the explanation?

The thing being explained, "value," is the price Pippin gets for the pin—$P. The explanation is that $P is a function of something called "labor." "Labor," according to the theory, seems to be a homogeneous, quantifiable entity. $P reflects the amount of labor involved in producing the pin. If production required a bit more labor, then the price would be a little above $P. If a bit less labor, then the price would be a little below $P.

The name of the theory suggests that the quantity of labor figures importantly into prices—so importantly that, rather than a "cost theory of value" or "inputs theory of value," it is a "*labor* theory of value."

If we buy into the assumption of a dominant and homogeneous input called "labor," it is reasonable to think that there would be usefulness in stories in which prices move with the amount of labor required.

But should we buy into that assumption? What is this homogeneous input called "labor"? In what sense, if any, is labor homogeneous?

Pippin's pins help us ponder things Adam Smith wrote in the *Wealth of Nations*, such as the following:

> Labour, therefore, it appears evidently, is the only universal, as well as the only accurate measure of value, or the only standard by which we can compare the values of different commodities at all times and at all places. (WN 54.17)

> In this state of things, the whole produce of labour belongs to the labourer; and the quantity of labour commonly employed in acquiring or producing any commodity, is the only circumstance which can regulate the quantity of labour which it ought commonly to purchase, command, or exchange for. (WN 65.4)

Adam Smith's supposed labor theory of value (LTV) is famously controversial. Drawing on an article in *Journal of Economic Behavior and Organization* (Robinson and Subrick 2021), we propose that he knew that the labor theory of value provided no explanation at all for the determination of prices. Smith understood that utility and scarcity played fundamental roles, as evidenced by his own *Lectures on Jurisprudence* (LJ). He recognized the heterogeneity of labor, the division of labor, the importance of ingenuity and knowledge asymmetries, and the importance of factors, such as land, that cannot be reduced to labor.

We argue that Smith saw these pitfalls of the LTV, but used it as a noble lie to affirm the moral value of labor and argue that it receives fair compensation in a market-based economy. He emphasized the importance of labor in establishing moral claims to property and uses the labor theory to defend his liberal plan. However, by way of his weak defense of the LTV, he implicitly consigned it to a merely symbolic role in economic discourse.

In developing our interpretation, we have been greatly influenced by William Rodney Herring and Mark Garrett Longaker's article "Wishful, Rational, and Political Thinking: The Labor Theory of Value" (2014), which suggests that the emphasis on labor in John Locke's theory and the LTV in classical economics was, essentially, a rhetorical ploy for selling the free market. We find ourselves largely sympathetic to Herring and Longaker, but perhaps more favorable than they to what is being sold.

The Labor Theory Muddle

In Book 1, Chapter 6 of *Wealth of Nations* (WN), Smith proposes the LTV:

> In that early and rude state of society... the proportion between the quantities of labour necessary for acquiring different objects seems to be the only circumstance which can afford any rule for exchanging them for one another. If among a nation of hunters, for example, it usually costs twice the labour to kill a beaver which it does to kill a deer, one beaver should naturally exchange for or be worth two deer. It is natural that what is usually the produce of two days or two hours labour, should be worth double of what is usually the produce of one day's or one hour's labour. (WN 65.1)

Smith first advances a LTV and then immediately complicates matters by acknowledging that "some allowance will naturally be made for... superior hardship... [or] an uncommon degree of dexterity and ingenuity." (WN 65.2-3) Even in the "rudest state" of society, labor is *not* homogeneous. Smith writes:

> In the advanced state of society, allowances of this kind, for superior hardship and superior skill, are commonly made in the wages of labour; **and something of the same kind must probably have taken place in its earliest and rudest period.** (WN 65.3, emphasis added)

Smith complicates matters further by denying that labor is the ultimate source of value for the profits of stock, rendering "a strict LTV untenable" (Shliesser, 2022). He explicitly denies the thought that "the profits of stock... are only a different name for the wages of a particular sort of labor" (WN 66.6). Smith 's labor theory does not offer a clear explanation or meaning of the concept of "natural price." These many complications in Smith's theory have led to a wide diversity of interpretations and difficulties in understanding his ideas.

Varied Interpretations

There are many variations of the LTV, but Smith's ideas do not comfortably fit into any of them. The three most plausible interpretations of Smith's words contain sufficient inconsistencies to suggest to us that he never earnestly advanced a LTV. Additionally, Smith knew of and acknowledged alternative approaches to the question of price determination. Therefore, it seems likely that Smith emphasized labor in his discussions for rhetorical rather than for analytical purposes.

The first possible interpretation of Smith's words is that he is suggesting a way to compare the earnings of a worker at different points in time. This interpretation suggests that Smith is using the labor of a worker earning average wages as a method of comparison, but not as a theory to explain price.

The second possible interpretation is that labor was more homogeneous in the past, and therefore could be used to determine price (or terms of trade, in barter) in a single special case. But Smith immediately acknowledges that even in the earliest state of society, the value of labor varies somewhat from individual to individual, as we discussed above. Instead of a theory of relative prices, perhaps the original homogeneity of labor is the basis for a moral norm surrounding toil and pain, and the rules of justice in exchange. Smith leaves this notion undeveloped and points to market forces to sort out relative prices, noting that the ordinary market price is "sufficient for carrying on the business of common life" (WN, 49.4).

The third possible interpretation of Smith's words is that he is proposing a cost of production model in which all value ultimately arises out of labor. However, it makes little sense to reduce all costs of production to some form of labor, such as the labor of improving one's judgment or thinking up a new idea. This would only introduce more heterogeneity in labor. Furthermore, this interpretation assumes knowledge of the scenes and histories of labor, which is impossible to obtain or establish as common knowledge among readers.

Smith's successors David Ricardo and Karl Marx, criticized him for confusing the labor commanded by a product and the labor embodied in its production. Joseph Schumpeter (1954, 310) noted that it is understandable that later economists misunderstood Smith's meaning. Schumpeter argued that Smith uses labor to explain value only in the special case of the "early and rude state" of nature. According to Schumpeter, Smith made a muddle of things by treating labor as focal throughout his discussion.

Mark Blaug (1997, 51) argued that Smith was not promoting any sort of LTV, but was instead primarily concerned with marking a contrast between his own view and that of the mercantilists, who claimed that wealth consists of money itself. Both Blaug and Schumpeter promote an interpretation that Smith never intended to promote, for modern conditions, any sort of LTV.

Alternatively, some scholars argue that the LTV was a coherent part of Smith's broader philosophy. Terry Peach (2009) argues that Smith never intended to confine the labor theory to the "earliest and rudest" state and that his frequent appeals to labor in other sections of WN suggest that he genuinely intended to point to expended labor as the underlying determinant of exchangeable value.

Jeffrey Young (1997) suggests that Smith's underlying jurisprudential theory justifies a LTV in the early and rude state but also explains why Smith seemingly abandons the LTV as he espouses something more like a cost-of-production theory of value. In this interpretation, Smith's theory of value is tied closely to his theory of justice, and both rely on the judgment of the impartial spectator. In the early and rude state, the impartial spectator sympathizes with the pain and toil associated with labor. As the impartial spectator naturally sympathizes with expectations and the conditions of property, the value of a thing incorporates more than simply labor, which becomes increasingly heterogeneous. In developed society, the impartial spectator considers additional factors, such as risk and possession. Smith's theory is internally coherent, Young argues, but in a non-obvious way for economists who ignore Smith's jurisprudence and moral theory. We feel that there is merit in Young's interpretation but that he does not give sufficient consideration to Smith's words, in boldface in a quotation above, where Smith himself subverts the assumption that labor was ever homogeneous.

A New Interpretation

We conjecture that Smith recognized the incoherence of a LTV and employed the language as a sort of noble lie to advance his liberal plan for society. We argue that Smith would have known of an alternative explanation for value, such as the role of scarcity and subjective desires in determining value, as outlined in LJ. We also claim that Smith may have had good reason to shroud or otherwise deemphasize this alternative explanation of value in his magnum opus.

In LJ, Smith follows closely the arguments about utility and scarcity found in his predecessors, Samuel Pufendorf and Gershom Carmichael. He demonstrates awareness about the demand side of value. Indeed, Smith's early work, *The Theory of Moral Sentiments*, elaborates the role of individual estimations in the determination of aesthetic and moral values.

Furthermore, Smith placed great emphasis on the heterogeneity of labor in WN, referring frequently to *productive* labor "which adds value of the subject upon which it is bestowed" in contrast to *unproductive* labor which does not (WN, 331.1). This implies that Smith held a more sophisticated view of the relationship between labor and wages. He emphasized the importance of the division of labor and its associated heterogeneity in raising productivity in a nation, rather than relying solely on a LTV to explain the source of prosperity.

Smith writes of a "rude state of society in which there is no division of labour" (WN 276.1). In that world, there is limited trade and people have no reason to save or build surplus stocks for exchange. The rude state of society fades as people realize gains from trade which arise from specialization. But with trade comes increasingly heterogeneous skillsets.

Once people recognize the gains from trade that arise from specialization, it is discovered that some are better at producing goods and services than others. With the addition of physical capital as well as human capital, labor productivity increases. Workers produce much more than they can based solely on their labor. This process of specialization leads to a virtuous circle of increased prosperity.

Smith's system of natural liberty emphasizes the importance of institutions in creating value, rather than labor alone. It relies on competition to promote the well-being of the laboring classes by expanding trading opportunities and increasing productivity. No longer did they have only one person to whom to sell their labor or goods. As the market size grew, the ability to walk away from some opportunities offered a source of self-respect and "independency" (WN, 378, 399, 402). Increased trading opportunities provide power to laborers.

Smith expresses his sympathy for the laborer who, when gathering the natural fruits of nature "when land was in common, cost the labourer only the trouble of gathering them... [and who now] must then pay for the license to gather them; and must give up to the landlord a portion of what his labour either collects or produces" (WN, 67). Smith recognized that employers and laborers sometimes have unequal bargaining power. He observed that employers sometimes attempt to collude to lower the wages of their workers. A partial solution to this problem is competition, which provides workers with broader opportunity sets and exit options that discipline employers and raise real wages.

Dignified Labor

We conjecture that Smith used the language of the labor theory of value as a rhetorical tool to promote his liberal ideas of society, while recognizing the incoherence of the theory itself. He does this through a subtle, pedagogical method by which he enters into the received opinions of his time and points out the contradictions within them, ultimately making a case for the dignity of the laboring classes (see

Melzer 2014, 216).

WN is a work of rhetoric as well as a treatise of economic principles. Smith writes in WN:

> The property which every man has in his own labour, as it is the original foundation of all other property, so it is the most sacred and inviolable. The patrimony of a poor man lies in the strength and dexterity of his hands; and to hinder him from employing this strength and dexterity in what manner he thinks proper without injury to his neighbour, is a plain violation of this most sacred property. (WN 138.12)

Smith made the case that the division of labor, within the right institutional settings, would produce prosperity for the laboring classes. Smith understood that as society progressed to the commercial age, labor became more complex and heterogeneous, but people's beliefs and norms did not keep pace with these changes. Smith used the language of LTV in WN to assure the laboring classes that their labor remained dignified and rewarded under his liberal plan. He employed a kind of esotericism, suggesting some kind of LTV to express a belief in the dignity of labor—a belief that was sincere.

References

Blaug, Mark. 1997. *Economic Theory in Retrospect*. Cambridge: Cambridge University Press.

Herring, Rodney H., and Mark Garrett Longaker. 2014. Wishful, Rational, and Political Thinking: The Labor Theory of Value as Rhetoric. *Argumentation and Advocacy* 50(4): 193-209.

Melzer, Arthur M. 2014. *Philosophy Between the Lines: The Lost History of Esoteric Writing*. Chicago: University of Chicago Press.

Peach, Terry. 2009. Adam Smith and the Labor Theory of (Real) Value: A Reconsideration. *History of Political Economy* 41(2): 383-406.

Robinson, John A., and J. Robert Subrick. 2021. Why Did Smith Suggest a Labor Theory of Value? *Journal of Economic Behavior and Organization* 184: 781–787.

Schumpeter, Joseph A. (1954). History of Economic Analysis. United Kingdom: Routledge.

Shliesser, Eric. 2022. Smith's Labor Theory Thought Experiment. *Adam Smith Works*, October 12.

Smith, Adam.1982 (LJ). *Lectures on Jurisprudence*, eds. R.L. Meek, D.D. Raphael, and P.G. Stein. Oxford: Oxford University Press.

Smith, Adam. 1976 [1776] (WN). *An Inquiry Into the Nature and Causes of The Wealth of Nations*, eds. R. H. Campbell and A. S. Skinner, 2 vols. Oxford: Oxford University Press.

Smith, Adam. 1976 [1790]. *The Theory of Moral Sentiments*, eds. D. D. Raphael and A. L. Macfie. Oxford: Oxford University Press.

Young, Jeffrey. 1997. *Economics as a Moral Science*. Cheltenham: Edward Elgar.

CHAPTER 15

Parmenides Addresses Plato, as Adam Smith Addresses Us

Jon Murphy and Andrew Humphries

We published a scholarly article entitled "His Memory Has Misled Him? Two Supposed Errors in Adam Smith's *Theory of Moral Sentiments*," in the *Journal of Economic Behavior and Organization* (2021). In that article we address two supposed errors in Smith's *Theory of Moral Sentiments* (TMS). Here we tell about one supposed error. We suggest that Smith might have made the seeming error on purpose.

Responding to a misconception about his theory of moral sentiments, namely, that it implies that the sentiment of the crowd or "the community" is the standard of praiseworthiness, Smith writes, on the contrary,

> To a real wise man the judicious and well-weighed approbation of a single wise man, gives more heartfelt satisfaction than all the noisy applauses of ten thousand ignorant though enthusiastic admirers.

He illustrates his point with a story about Parmenides addressing Plato:

He [the real wise man] may say with Parmenides, who, upon reading a philosophical discourse before a public assembly at Athens, and observing, that, except Plato, the whole company had left him, continued, notwithstanding, to read on, and said that Plato alone was audience sufficient for him. (TMS, 253.31)

The approbation of one wise man, Plato, not the noisy applause of ignorant admirers, was sufficient for Parmenides.

But no such meeting between Plato and Parmenides could have occurred. And Smith surely knew that.

Parmenides was approximately 88 years older than Plato. If Parmenides had addressed Plato aged 20, Parmenides would have to have been 108!

Smith, in his *History of Astronomy* (p. 53), calls Parmenides an "antesocratic sage," indicating that he knew that Parmenides was a pre-Socratic. Moreover, Smith was surely familiar with the dialogue titled *Parmenides* by Plato, and he was well aware of a uniqueness of that dialogue: In *Parmenides*, Socrates is but a tyro, and a diffident auditor, while Parmenides plays the role of the senior philosopher and authority. Anyone mindful of the dialogue *Parmenides* would be able to see that there is no way that Plato could have met Parmenides. It is extremely unlikely that the impossibility of Plato meeting Parmenides could have escaped Smith: Plato is both the author of *Parmenides* and auditor of Parmenides, in Smith's story. Smith is winking at us!

Parmenides might be able to address Plato—or us—in spirit. But of course, Smith knew that Parmenides could not have addressed Plato in the flesh.

A general reader today might not recognize how ahistorical the story is, but it would be analogous to writing of Adam Smith lecturing to John Stuart Mill! In fact, the difference between Mill's birth-year of 1806 and Smith's of 1723 is 83 years, less than that between Parmenides and Plato.

The editors of TMS, D.D. Raphael and A.L. Macfie recognize the problem and cite the corrected story, but account for it as a lapse of memory:

> Smith's memory has misled him. Cicero, *Brutus*, li.91, tells the story about Antimachus reading a long poem before an audience that eventually consisted only of Plato. The philosopher Parmenides (even if in his old age he met the young Socrates, as Plato's dialogue *Parmenides* supposes) must have died before Plato was born. (TMS, 253 n.27)

Smith thus makes two changes to the story: he substitutes Parmenides for Antimachus and "a philosophical discourse" for a poem. Smith knew his Cicero. How could Smith make such blunders?

In *Philosophy Between the Lines: The Lost History of Esoteric Writing*, Arthur Melzer explains that "implausible blunders," "errors of fact," and "misquotations" have been common techniques of esoteric writing (Melzer, 2014, 55). Although Smith was writing near the close of the period in which esoteric writing was accepted as common, and although Smith is unusual in seeming to deny the existence of esoteric writing (*History of Ancient Logics and Metaphysics*, 121-123n*; Melzer, 2014, 28), there is some interest in ways in which Smith might have written esoterically, at least indirectly and ironically. Smith may have written in ways to make his views more acceptable and politically palatable than he could have achieved by being more direct (see Klein & Merrill, 2021). One purpose of esotericism, Melzer explains, is pedagogical—giving hints and making the reader ponder the matter more deeply, as in the Socratic method. If Smith did intentionally alter the story as told by Cicero, it makes sense to see it as pedagogical esotericism.

If intentional, what might have been Smith's motive in misrepresenting the story?

First, the story illustrates the contrast between the approval of an undiscerning crowd and a discerning individual. Smith's moral and aesthetic theory emphasizes the idea that man wants, not only to be approved of, but to be worthy of approval. And this worthiness is measured, not by the approval of just anyone, but by a wise, informed, and impartial spectator.

There are several moments in TMS in which Smith's shows great admiration for Plato. Smith associates Plato with the most extensive sense of justice—estimative justice (TMS, 270). Estimative justice is estimating or evaluating an object or idea with a degree of esteem of which it is due, and pursuing it accordingly.

Smith's substitution of a philosopher (Parmenides) for Antimachus (a poet), and a philosophical discourse for of a poem as the object that is estimated by the auditor, Plato, supports the idea that Smith intended the story to be a wink that would draw special attention to his own philosophical work as the object of estimation. We think it is reasonable to think Smith is saying "I seek the approval of the most virtuous. That is the judge one should seek." Smith is reiterating that his moral system does not depend on the crowd.

Second, Cicero tells us that Antimachus' poem was deliberately aimed at a few wise men rather than the throng. In Cicero's original telling of the story, Antimachus' poem is full of obscure allusions that only a few will appreciate. Might Smith have been riffing on this part of the story as an obscure allusion to speak to those who are most knowledgeable and critical in the history of philosophy? Might he have been inviting his own readers to consider: For whom is Smith writing? The assent of the throng, or the approbation of the few? Who really is the wise man?

Finally, Smith has Plato judge Parmenides, although they could not have been contemporaries. By imagining that such thinkers meet out of time, Smith may have been signaling that it is not the actual approval of any living man that he most deeply desired. The wise man seeks to be thought worthy by the best judges, those who would or ought to approve of our work, conduct, and character, no matter when that person is to be found. In other words, proper approval comes not simply from *living* spectators, but higher spectators who may be across time or even *outside of* time.

If the interpretations that we are offering here have merit, there then arises another question, and one we do not attempt to address here. Smith takes the story from Cicero and erases Antimachus. Smith could have put any number of "antesocratic" philosophers in his place. Why Parmenides? In selecting Parmenides, was Smith telling us something about what he thought of Parmenides teachings? Was Smith telling us something about how Parmenides relates to Plato?

We are not prepared to address the "Why Parmenides?" question. We can say, however, that Parmenides was respected in his own time and seems to have been highly influential on Plato. Smith seems to be positing that Parmenides would have recognized Plato's wisdom and sought his approval as a wise judge. Do not settle for the approval of the crowd. Search for the approval of sages in time to come.

It is, of course, possible that, as Raphael and Macfie suggested, Smith merely erred. But we find it very unlikely Smith would have changed the story by mistake. We also think it worthwhile to think through how this seeming error might have been something of a playful and even poignant wink to his readers. In any case, Smith's story reminds us that our sentiments are to be judged not by the throng, or even necessarily by our contemporaries, but by a higher judge. Our sentiments and actions necessarily take place in the context of our time and place, but when we act and when we judge the praiseworthiness of our actions and our sentiments, we should think beyond the here and now and ask that eternal question: am I doing good in the eyes of an ideal impartial spectator, or am I just appearing to do so to ignorant though enthusiastic admirers?

References

Klein, Daniel B., and Thomas W. Merrill. 2021. Adam Smith, David Hume, Liberalism, and Esotericism: Introduction. *Journal of Economic Behavior & Organization* 184: 712-716.

Melzer, Arthur M. 2014. *Philosophy Between the Lines: The Lost History of Esoteric Writing*. Chicago: University of Chicago Press

Murphy, Jon, and Andrew Humphries. 2021. His Memory Has Misled Him? Two Supposed Errors in Adam Smith's *Theory of Moral Sentiments*. *Journal of Economic Behavior & Organization* 184: 771-780.

Smith, Adam. 1980. *Essays on Philosophical Subjects*. Indianapolis: Liberty Fund, Inc.

Smith, Adam. 1982 (1759). *The Theory of Moral Sentiments*. Indianapolis: Liberty Fund, Inc.

CHAPTER 16

French Liberal Economics, 1695–1776

Benoît Malbranque

Economic liberalism was formulated over several generations of intellectuals across Europe. The contribution of France was especially valuable from the year 1695.

At that time, for reasons historic and geographic, a centralized and warrior state, greedy for taxes, had risen in France. Under Louis XIV, extreme luxury in Versailles offered a striking contrast to the grimy and endemic misery of the countryside, which only worsened during times of extreme weather and bad harvests, like in 1695.

Some exceptional figures not only offered practical solutions, primarily tax reform, but ventured into economic principles. In his peculiar prose, Pierre de Boisguilbert argued for the urgency of abolishing the current tax system, said to be arbitrary and disastrous, but he also examined the unintended consequences of such measures as trade barriers and price control on grain. Boisguilbert allowed that such measures might have been well-intended. He maintained, however, that they were nonetheless oppressive by their very nature. He then explained how freedom and competition could produce a state of harmony and general prosperity. A summary of his economic ideas can be found in his motto, "let nature run its course." He moved to erect the principle of non-intervention into a system of public policy (Boisguilbert 1695, 1705).

Around the same time, Marshal Vauban, a military man, inspired both by an interest in statistics and a real love for humanity, similarly understood the disincentive nature of arbitrary taxation. He advocated the elimination of virtually all taxes in favor of a single flat-rate contribution based on several sort of revenues (Vauban 1707).

The economic themes of Vauban and Boisguilbert were amplified by such authors as the abbot de Saint-Pierre, a lover of peace and humanity, who devoted himself to the continuous improvement of society. Saint-Pierre authored numerous proposals that he termed "projects," which were later appreciated by Gustave de Molinari (Molinari 1857). Throughout these proposals of Saint-Pierre, one finds clear expression of many economic principles such as that trade, operating freely, is positive-sum (Saint-Pierre 1733, vol. 5, 173).

The influence of these early figures was, however, limited. Saint-Pierre was called a dreamer, Boisguilbert a madman, and Vauban was harassed until his death. Ministers remained deaf and blind to the new perspectives on commerce. They sought expedients and proposed new forms of economic controls. One, introduced by John Law, resulted in a collapse—the so-called Mississippi Bubble (1718-1720)—that encouraged able minds to enquire into its causes and beyond.

Jean-François Melon and the mysterious Du Tot analyzed, in treatises of wider scope, the effects of the debasement of money, which played a key role in the collapse of Law's scheme. Richard Cantillon—born in Ireland, he became French in 1708—offered one of the very first systems of economic reasoning, in which entrepreneurship, private property and individual initiative were key (Cantillon 1755). Economic discussions were becoming popular. In the middle of the 18th century, Montesquieu examined economic affairs with his usual superior point of view, but offered principles sometimes unsound and unaligned with the liberal line.

In the meantime, other Europeans countries had made significant progress, both in economic development and in economic discourse. Seeing France falling behind, Vincent de Gournay organized a large translation effort involving a group of literary men. He undertook translations himself, wrote occasionally, and invited others to write and publish. Two of his memorials against the exclusionary privileges of guilds have been translated into English (Gournay 1753). While his appeals remained, like Cantillon's and Melon's, rooted in mercantilist rhetoric about national greatness and power, Gournay nonetheless promoted the complete freedom of work, over against the guild system. His pupils, Turgot and Morellet would remember him fondly as a teacher of laissez-faire (Turgot, 1759; Morellet 1821, I, 36-37).

The brilliance of the marquis d'Argenson, like that of Gournay, can only be measured retrospectively. D'Argenson wrote memorials and several volumes of journal notes, which were rediscovered much later; similarly, his main work on government (*Considérations sur le gouvernement*), first disseminated in a manuscript form, was published only after his death. If, with his great sense of humanity, he echoed his old mentor Saint-Pierre in some respects, his economic principles were sharper and more radical: non-intervention, complete free-trade, and a limited government. Free competition, he argues, will ensure a degree of common prosperity that government planning can never achieve (d'Argenson 1742; d'Argenson 1765, 185; d'Argenson 1751, 109-110; d'Argenson 1765, 41). Without knowing each other personally, Gournay and d'Argenson found themselves in agreement (d'Argenson 1755).

While Boisguilbert, Vauban, and Saint-Pierre each spoke out as somewhat isolated voices, the common effort of Gournay, d'Argenson, and others fostered a current of lively liberal discourse. Once very rare, economic publications had become common and widespread.

During the early 1750s, the doctor François Quesnay, alone in Versailles, discontinued his study of medicine for that of political economy. In 1756, the marquis de Mirabeau obtained great celebrity with his curious book *L'Ami des Hommes*, and from 1757 onwards, Quesnay and Mirabeau join forces. Dupont, Baudeau, Le Trosne, and many others, soon after joined their cause.

In the early 1760s, such figures recognized the urgency of disseminating this new science; they gathered and joined forces. Due to a great variety of backgrounds, personalities and even ideas, the so-called physiocrat school was really a plural society with blurry boundaries. The term "physiocracy" was not significant to the group at the time, and the subsequent employment of that label by intellectual historians and commentators is cause for regret.

Quesnay was an old man, as though a grandparent to young men in the set like Dupont de Nemours; Mirabeau was an aristocrat, and Roubaud a self-made man from very humble roots. Quesnay entered political economy as a doctor, Dupont as a poet, Abeille and Le Trosne as lawyers.

If we go beyond Quesnay's *Tableau Économique* and the debate on the exclusive productivity of lands (and waters), which is mainly a verbal matter, these economists put forward some key principles. They described theoretically why central direction fails (Abeille 1763, 13-14; Abeille 1768, 45; Le Trosne 1768b, 15-19 et 52; Mirabeau 1768; Turgot 1773). They argue that, in a system of free competition, self-interest will be a driving force bringing common prosperity (Mirabeau 1763, 50; Le Mercier de la Rivière 1767, 33, 35; Le Trosne 1768a, 193-194; Le Trosne 1768b, 36-37).

The conclusion of their studies and works is usually quite radical. They present it using the famous words "laissez faire, laissez passer," that is: Do not restrict economic activity (Baudeau 1771, 208-209; Le Trosne 1768b, 158, 168). Having little taste for compromise, they argue for "complete," "unlimited," "full and comprehensive" freedom of trade (Abeille 1768, 55;Le Trosne 1768a, 155; Le Trosne 1768b, 9). Their view on the role of government is that it should be minimal (Le Trosne 1768, 58-59; Le Trosne 1777, 69-70). Le Trosne, a rather overlooked figure, leads the fight against "monopolies of every sort, of every size, of every aspect and color" (Le Trosne 1766, 23). He argues that free trade, even unilaterally, is beneficial.

One can only regret the lack of a proper treatise on economics in their common legacy. Quesnay was working and living in the palace of Versailles, and could not have dreamt of it—besides, his mental abilities were declining; Turgot was in government and found the time to pen only a "sketch." The sort of economic journalism of Dupont, Baudeau, Abeille and Le Trosne can be explained by their conviction that "a science as new and as far-reaching as economics can only be treated at first part by part" (Le Trosne 1767). This mindset gave rise to a diffuse array of writings, whose access today is difficult, although rewarding. For example, in 1907, Gustave Schelle (355) compared the forgotten Le Trosne to Bastiat himself. Le Trosne wrote some delightful pieces, such as the "Request of the Carriers of Orléans," which, three-quarter of a century before the "Petition of the Candlemakers," is similarly an instructive mockery (Le Trosne 1765b; Le Trosne 1766, 246; Le Trosne 1768a, 126).

Alongside the circle that has come to be termed "the physiocrats" were men defending similar ideas, fellow travelers, including Morellet, Turgot, Condillac, Condorcet, and Chastellux. The abbot Morellet was introduced to political economy before the rise of the physiocrats, and he outlived all of them; yet his economic works are as fragmentary as theirs. He engaged into a large but never completed *Dictionary of Commerce*, and started translating Adam Smith's *Wealth of Nations* without ever finishing. Many of his publications on economics are filled, nonetheless, with great insights, like the well-named

Fragment of a Letter on the Grain Trade Question (Morellet 1764). In another rushed publication, he advanced a rights-based defense of liberalism (Morellet 1770, 103-104), and fellow liberal economists likewise mounted ethical arguments for liberty (Abeille 1765, 33; Le Trosne 1768b, 116).

Turgot's brilliance flashed in writings of a life busy and cut short at age 54. In the middle of a tiring enquiry he was conducting in his province, he wrote some insightful letters on the freedom of trade in just three weeks, (Dupont 1808, vol. 6, 119; Condorcet 1786, 49). Similarly, he prepared some *Reflexions on the Formation and Distribution of Wealth* to be distributed to two Chinese who were travelling back to their country. What would he have published if he had moved in with his mother and meditated ten years by the warm chimney?

In 1776, at last, liberal economic thought in France, scattered but remarkable, found expression in a treatise on economics. In a letter addressed to lord Shelburne, dated April 12th 1776, and alongside which was sent a copy of the new book, "filled with good reasoning," by Condillac, *Le Commerce et le Gouvernement* (On commerce and government), Morellet explains that he has just received the first volume of Adam Smith, where there are also very good principles, amidst developments "perhaps rather long," a sign of an ill that he calls "*scotish subtilty*" (Morellet 1776). There finally appeared, on both side of the Channel, major statements of thinking advanced by many generations of economists across Europe.

The history of economic liberalism in France from 1695 to 1776 deserves a single treatment, large and colorful. Without question there is a common legacy, a rich French source to what Peter Boettke calls the historic mainline of economic thought—the liberal line. A large treatment of the French wellsprings would unfold powerful economic reasoning, but also communicate a mindset of humanity, tolerance, and openness.

References

Abeille, Louis-Paul. 1763. *Lettre d'un négociant sur la nature du commerce des grains.*

Abeille, Louis-Paul. 1765. *Effets d'un privilège exclusif en matière de commerce, sur les droits de la propriété, etc.* Paris: Regnard.

Abeille, Louis-Paul. 1768. *Principes sur la liberté du commerce des grains,* Paris: Desaint.

Argenson, René Louis de Voyer de Paulmy. 1742. Mémoire à composer pour délibérer par le pour et le contre, et décider que la France devrait laisser l'entrée et la sortie libres dans le royaume de toutes marchandises nationales et étrangères, sans prendre aucuns droits royaux, mettant tous ces droits sur les consommations par voies sûres pour éviter la fraude. (Juillet 1742).

Argenson, René Louis de Voyer de Paulmy. 1751. "Lettre à l'auteur du Journal œconomique au sujet de la Dissertation sur le commerce de M. le Marquis Belloni," *Journal Œconomique,* Avril 1751. Paris: Boudet.

Argenson, René Louis de Voyer de Paulmy. 1755. Journal, entry for the date April 17th, 1755. Bibliothèque universitaire de Poitiers. Archives d'Argenson.

Argenson, René Louis de Voyer de Paulmy. 1765. *Considérations sur le gouvernement ancien et présent de la France,* Amsterdam: Rey (fake; Paris).

Boisguilbert, Pierre de. [1695]. *Le Détail de la France. La cause de la diminution de ses biens, et la facilité du remède, en fournissant en un mois tout l'argent dont le Roi a besoin et enrichissant tout le monde.*

Boisguilbert, Pierre de. 1705. "Factum de la France contre les demandeurs en délai pour l'exécution du projet traité dans le Détail de la France ou le nouvel ambassadeur arrivé du pays du peuple," Archives du ministère des affaires étrangères, France 1138 / Affaires intérieures 398, 1705, fol. 79- 220.

Cantillon, Richard. 1755. [Posthumously published by Gournay] *Essai sur la nature du commerce en général.* "À Londres, Chez Fletcher Gyles, dans Holborn" (fake; Paris).

Condorcet, Jean Antoine Nicolas de Caritat de. 1786. *Vie de Monsieur Turgot.* Londres (fake: Paris).

Gournay, Jean Claude Marie, Vincent de. 1753. Mémoire sur les manufactures de Lyon. Bibliothèque municipale de Lyon, Fonds Matthieu Bonafous, Ms 6055, f° 10–33.

Le Trosne, Guillaume-François. 1765a. "Lettre sur les avantages du commerce des vaisseaux étrangers pour la voiture de nos grains," *Journal de l'agriculture, du commerce et des finances,* août 1765, p. 45-122. Paris: Knapen.

Le Trosne, Guillaume-François. 1765b. Requête des rouliers d'Orléans. *Journal de l'agriculture, du commerce et des finances,* t. III, troisième partie, décembre 1765, p.56-85. Paris: Knapen.

Le Trosne, Guillaume-François. 1766. "Lettre sur l'utilité des discussions économiques," *Journal de l'agriculture, du commerce et des finances,* tome VI, première partie, juillet 1766, Paris: Knapen.

Le Trosne, Guillaume-François. 1767. Lettre à M. Tscharner, secrétaire de la Société économique de Berne. Orléans, 7 janvier 1767. Bibliothèque de la Bourgeoisie (Burgerbibliothek), Berne, Suisse: Fonds d'archives de la Société économique de Berne (Oekonomische Gesellschaft).

Le Trosne, Guillaume-François. 1768a. *Recueil de plusieurs morceaux économiques*, Paris: Desaint.

Le Trosne, Guillaume-François. 1768b. *Lettres à un ami, sur les avantages de la liberté du commerce des grains et le danger des prohibitions*, Paris: Desaint.

Le Mercier de la Rivière, Pierre-Paul. 1767. *L'Ordre naturel et essentiel des sociétés politiques*. Paris: Desaint.

Mirabeau, Victor Riquetti de. 1763. *Philosophie rurale, ou Économie générale et politique de l'agriculture réduite à l'ordre immuable des lois physiques et morales qui assurent la prospérité des empires*, Amsterdam (fake; Paris).

Mirabeau, Victor Riquetti de. 1768. "Projet d'édit sur le commerce des grains". Archives nationales de France, Fonds Quesnay-Mirabeau, M. 784, n°3.

Morellet, André. 1764. *Fragment d'une lettre sur la police des grains*. Bruxelles (fake; Paris).

Morellet, André. 1776. Lettre à lord Shelburne, Paris, 12 avril 1776. British Library, Lansdowne and Shelburne Papers, MS carton 24.

Morellet, André. 1821. *Mémoires inédits sur le dix-huitième siècle et sur la révolution*, Paris: Ladvocat.

Molinari, Gustave de. 1857. *L'abbé de Saint-Pierre, membre exclu de l'Académie française: sa vie et ses œuvres, précédées d'une appréciation et d'un précis historique de l'idée de la paix perpétuelle*. Paris: Guillaumin.

Saint-Pierre, Charles-Irénée Castel de. 1733. "Projet pour perfectionner le commerce de France," *Ouvrages de politique*, t. V, Paris: Briasson.

Schelle, Gustave. 1907. *Le docteur Quesnay: chirurgien, médecin de Mme de Pompadour et de Louis XV, physiocrate*. Paris: Félix Alcan.

Turgot, Anne-Robert-Jacques. 1759. Éloge de Gournay. *Mercure de France*, août 1759.

Turgot, Anne-Robert-Jacques. 1773. Lettre à l'abbé Terray sur la marque des fers. Limoges, 24 décembre 1773.

Vauban, Sébastien Le Prestre de. 1707. *Projet d'une dîme royale, qui supprimant la taille, les aides, les douanes d'une province à l'autre, les décimes du Clergé, les affaires extraordinaires, et tous autres impôts onéreux et non volontaires, et diminuant le prix du sel de moitié et plus, produirait au Roi un revenu certain et suffisant, sans frais, et sans être à charge à l'un de ses sujets plus qu'à l'autre, qui s'augmenterait considérablement par la meilleure culture des terres*.

CHAPTER 17

The Courts of Princes and the Marketplace of Equals: Two Institutional Settings for the Cultivation of Virtue in Smith's Thought

Jordan J. Ballor

"In the courts of princes, in the drawing-rooms of the great...flattery and falsehood too often prevail...." — Adam Smith, *The Theory of Moral Sentiments*

Two different roads are presented to us," writes Adam Smith in a justly famous passage, "equally leading to the attainment of this so much desired object," that is, "to deserve, to acquire, and to enjoy the respect and admiration of mankind," which Smith says, "are the great objects of ambition and emulation."

Two different roads, says Smith, as well as "two different characters are presented to our emulation." He continues to extends the imagery: "Two different models, two different pictures, are held out to us, according to which we might fashion our own character and behavior."

These two different roads, characters, models, and pictures correspond to the two paths to attaining "the respect and admiration of mankind," or as he also puts it, the fulfilment of the "desire to be both respectable and to be respected," or praiseworthy and praised. One road is "the study of wisdom and the practice of virtue; the other [is] the acquisition of wealth and greatness."

Smith's discussion comes at the conclusion of an exploration of the origin of ranks and ambition in society and the corruption of our moral sentiments by a fundamental disposition of human nature in favor of the second road as opposed to the first, that is, our "disposition to admire the rich and the great."

But in addition to Smith's usage of the imagery of two alternatives, or we might say, a choice architecture, whether that be two roads or two characters, I want to bring attention to another element of Smith's discussion concerning what distinguishes these two options: a difference in institutional setting or context. One setting is princely courts, meaning both the space in which courtiers assembled and the courtiers themselves. (It was from this sense that the legal meaning of a tribunal for judicial investigation emerged.) The other setting is markets and commerce.

The two settings give rise to different tendencies in character and conduct, different ways of behaving. I call them *mores*, rather than morals or morality, because mores themselves can be better or worse. Mores do not necessarily deserve the sense of approval that "morals" and "morality" tend to suggest.

The courtly setting gives rise to what we might call "court mores," which deal with positional goods and relate to prestige, proximity to power, and the like. The other we might call "market mores," which have to do with mutual gain in exchange. To some extent, I think, Smith recognizes the legitimacy of each of these settings, but he judges that the scope of market mores should be expanded and court mores should be curtailed. There are tradeoffs, however, in both systems, tradeoffs that Smith acknowledges and reckons with. All of this has something to teach us today as we deal with the ongoing challenge to rightly order systems as they relate to the realities of both limited and positional goods as well as settings where mutual benefit and positive-sum exchanges are not only possible but ought to be encouraged.

Let's go back a bit in Smith's presentation to the discussion preceding the conclusion where he presents us with the two roads, to explore his treatment of two different institutional contexts for the cultivation of virtue and avoidance of vice, settings which inform his later conclusions regarding the compatibility of virtue and material gain in different institutional settings.

Court Mores

In his discussion "Of the origin of Ambition, and of the distinction of Ranks" in TMS, Smith describes the culture of power in his day. Those of material wealth, social power, and prestige, says Smith, offer "benefits [that] can extend to but a few; but their fortunes interest almost everybody." Even though practically speaking the largesse and favor of the rich and powerful can only directly impact few people, their way of life, their wealth, and their station receive near universal attention and concern.

Large-scale private enterprise was rare in Smith's time. We are accustomed to "the rich" including famous investors, inventor, and celebrities, and not necessarily implying political power and influence. In Smith's day, however, great wealth generally implied political power and influence. That needs to be kept in mind when reading his words concerning wealth and greatness.

As Smith continues his examination of the nobility and aristocratic society, he observes that it takes no special virtues or merit to maintain or ascend the ranks of social status: "By what important accomplishments is the young nobleman instructed to support the dignity of his rank, and to render himself worthy of that superiority over his fellow-citizens, to which the virtue of his ancestors had raised them? Is it by knowledge, by industry, by patience, by self-denial, or by virtue of any kind?" No, says Smith, it is by the destiny of birth that some have been placed into noble and aristocratic families, and their concerns are cultivated to conform to the norms, values, and mores of their class.

In this cultural setting, some are born to lead and to occupy the higher stations of life. Of the young nobleman, Smith says, "His air, his manner, his deportment, all mark that elegant and grateful sense of his own superiority, which those who are born to inferior stations can hardly ever arrive at. These are the arts by which he proposes to make mankind more easily submit to his authority, and to govern their inclinations according to his own pleasure; and in this he is seldom disappointed."

Smith apparently takes this phenomenon as natural, or at least typically characteristic of human societies. There are natural hierarchies, and these ranks, divisions, and classes may have different manifestations in different times and places. The phenomenon of the "distinction of ranks" by some standard, however, is universal in human society. Smith is well aware that governmental authority depends on focal points and conventions, and that differences in wealth, power, and family lineage provide focal points while differences in wisdom and virtue, "invisible and often uncertain," do not (TMS 226.20, see also 253.30, LJ 321–22, 402).

But elevation based on court mores by no means reflects merit. Smith illustrates the point with the Sun King, Louis XIV. On what basis has history judged Louis to be a great king? "Was it by his extensive knowledge, by his exquisite judgment, or by his heroic valour? It was by none of these qualities," Smith concludes. Instead, Louis excelled at the virtues that were necessary and appropriate in a courtly context. As Smith quotes one account of Louis' success, the king "surpassed all his courtiers in the gracefulness of his shape, and the majestic beauty of his features. The sound of his voice, noble and affecting, gained those hearts which his presence intimidated. He had a step and a deportment which could suit only him and his rank, and which would have been ridiculous in any other person."

The flair of aristocracy, or court mores, emphasizes one's presentation, deportment, style, and grace. Traditional virtues like bravery, prudence, knowledge, patience, self-denial, and the like, are largely irrelevant. Of Louis, Smith concludes that compared with the royal flair, "no other virtue, it seems appeared to have any merit. Knowledge, industry, valour, and beneficence, trembled, were abashed, and lost all dignity before them."

Smith goes so far as to say that in its vanity, court mores come to detest virtue: "All… the virtues which can fit, either for the council, the senate, or the field, are, by the insolent and insignificant flatterers, who commonly figure the most in such corrupted societies, held in the utmost contempt and derision."

Market Mores

As opposed to court mores, consider market or commercial mores. Whereas the men and women of rank and distinction are concerned with the cultivation of appearances, the human beings who operate within the marketplace must concern themselves with the cultivation of a whole host of virtues, some of which Smith has already identified in his list of those things that are absent from the halls of courtly power and prestige.

As Smith puts it, the distinction between court mores and market mores also corresponds to a distinction between the public and the private man. Of the private man, Smith writes, "The most perfect modesty and plainness, joined to as much negligence as is consistent with the respect due to the company, ought to be the chief characteristics of the behaviour of a private man." He continues:

> If [the private man] ever hopes to distinguish himself, it must be by more important virtues. He must acquire dependants to balance the dependants of the great, and he has no other fund to pay them from, but the labour of his body, and the activity of his mind. He must cultivate these therefore: he must acquire superior knowledge in his profession, and superior industry in the exercise of it. He must be patient in labour, resolute in danger, and firm in distress. These talents he must bring into public view, by the difficulty, importance, and, at the same time, good judgment of his undertakings, and by the severe and unrelenting application with which he pursues them. Probity and prudence, generosity and frankness, must characterize his behaviour upon all ordinary occasions. (TMS 55.5)

This is one summary of the character of those who excel in commercial and market settings as opposed to places where there is jockeying for position and proximity to political power and prerogative. Whereas court mores are characterized by hierarchy, aristocracy, privileges, positional competition, and tend to be zero-sum (because of their positional nature), market mores are characterized by a more egalitarian set of commercial virtues, expressed in a setting where mutually beneficial exchange is the norm. By reflecting on the setting, we come to understand what it is that tends to make the bourgeoisie more virtuous than courtiers.

The Contest between Court and Market Mores

Even though his presentation here in TMS of court mores is largely negative, it seems to me that Smith is not simply anti-aristocratic or anti-royalist. He is clear-eyed about the nature of court mores as a manifestation of institutional settings that run on contests for prestige, privilege, positional goods, and political power. It doesn't follow, however, that Smith thinks that we should seek to eradicate such features of human nature.

For Smith, the challenge seems to be, first, to rightly evaluate and, second, to develop a political economy that does justice to the natural inclinations of human beings to sort into ranks and classes while also expanding the sphere of mutually beneficial exchange.

What we can see in his evaluation of the two institutional settings as they inform the concluding imagery of two roads, characters, models, and pictures is that Smith wants to expand the scope and significance of market mores, where "more important virtues" like industriousness, thrift, honesty, temperance, and prudence can be cultivated more consistently and universally.

"In the middling and inferior stations of life," writes Smith, "the road to virtue and that to fortune, to such fortune, at least, as men in such stations can reasonably expect to acquire, are, happily, in most cases, very nearly the same." He continues, "In such situations, therefore, we may generally expect a considerable degree of virtue; and, fortunately for the good morals of society, these are the situations of by far the greater part of mankind." Markets and commercial societies are the institutional settings in which virtues are cultivated more consistently. "The good old proverb, therefore, that honesty is the best policy, holds, in such situations, almost always perfectly true." Much of Smith's later work in TMS as well as WN promotes the expansion of the settings that make honesty the best policy.

"In the superior stations of life the case is unhappily not always the same," Smith writes with obvious understatement. The emphasis in court mores on appearances over substance leads to the cultivation of lesser virtues, or even simulacra of virtue along with all kinds of vices. "In the courts of princes, in the drawing-rooms of the great," says Smith, "where success and preferment depend, not upon the esteem and intelligent and well-informed equals, but upon the fanciful and foolish favor of ignorant, presumptuous, and proud superiors; flattery and falsehood too often prevail over merit and abilities."

We can read Smith's larger project then as one in which he attempts to curtail court mores and expand market mores. And we can conclude with some words of wisdom for those of us born into the middling and inferior stations of life:

> Are you in earnest resolved never to barter your liberty for the lordly servitude of a court, but to live free, fearless, and independent? There seems to be one way to continue in that virtuous resolution; and perhaps but one. Never enter into the place from whence so few have been able to return; never come within the circle of ambition; nor ever bring yourself into comparison with those masters of the earth who have already engrossed the attention of half mankind before you. (TMS 57.7)

CHAPTER 18

Moral Innovation in Adam Smith

Dylan DelliSanti

T he impartiality of the impartial spectator—and of the related, though not synonymous, man within the breast—is one of the great controversies in Smith scholarship. Some scholars read into Smith's spectator the individualism of the early industrial age. For instance, Amartya Sen (2009, 125) writes that the impartial spectator, when evaluating an actor's conduct, can "go beyond reasoning...constrained by local conventions of thought, and to examine deliberately...what the accepted conventions would look like from the perspective of a 'spectator' at a distance."

Other scholars, however, have argued that the "man within the breast" is of limited use when it comes to seeing beyond our local conventions. Although the man within might encourage us to restrain our selfishness and conform to our society's standards, the man within cannot correct us if our society's standards are themselves flawed or hurtful. Samuel Fleischacker expresses this view:

> If the moral standards, the basic moral sentiments, of a
> society are profoundly corrupt—if a feeling of contempt
> for Africans or hatred for Jews or homosexuals, say, has
> been taken for a moral feeling, and a society's judgments of
> these people's actions have been comprehensively skewed

as a result—the impartial spectator within each individual will share in, rather than correcting for, that corruption. (Fleischacker 2011, 28-9)

If Fleischacker is correct, we might worry that Smith's moral system veers toward conformism, determinism, and relativism. We might be led to believe that Smith was pessimistic about the possibility that people could reform and amend the beliefs they inherit from their community. And indeed, when we dig into Smith's corpus, there is good reason to believe that he viewed humans as limited in amending received norms.

Humans are naturally sociable. We seek out the praise of our equals and we avoid becoming the subjects of their blame and censure. But, says Smith, we not only seek praise and avoid blame; we seek to be praiseworthy and avoid being blameworthy. That is, we seek to be worthy objects of praise, irrespective of the actual praise we receive. It would seem, then, that the impartial spectator as the arbiter of praise- and blame-worthiness might save humans from the circumstantial judgments of the community.

But Smith makes an important distinction between the impartial spectator and the man within the breast. Smith makes this distinction most apparent when talking of "the prudent man." When "the prudent man" sacrifices present pleasure for more substantial reward in the future, Smith writes that "the prudent man is always both supported and rewarded by the entire approbation of the impartial spectator, and of the representative of the impartial spectator, the man within the breast" (TMS, 215, italics added). The passage makes it quite clear that this impartial spectator is postulated by Smith as a universal being. This impartial spectator is postulated as a universal and accurate judge of praiseworthiness and blameworthiness. This impartial spectator is God or a God-like being.

We mere humans, however, must make do communicating with the impartial spectator through his representative—the man within the breast. We must thus understand how the man within is constructed. Smith is most explicit about the development of the man within in a series of passages I refer to as the "great school of self-command" section.

When we are toddlers, we feel little need to moderate our passions or partiality—our parents indulge our every sentiment. But when we first attend school, we find that our classmates "have no such indulgent partiality" (TMS, 145). For our own good, we moderate our selfishness to obtain their approval. It is here that we enter, what Smith calls, "the great school of self-command" (ibid). In the great school of self-command, we develop our man within the breast. We are constantly thinking about how our actions must look from the standpoint of a third-party. When we share our cookies and make a new friend, any praise makes an impression on our man within; when we steal Lego blocks and make an enemy, that scorn too makes an impression. By constantly taking in the feedback from real spectators, we gradually form a sense of praiseworthy and blameworthy conduct.

Our man within, it is clear, is partly the product of social construction. However, charges of moral determinism and relativism would be premature. For though we develop our man within through our interactions with society, everyone's man within is uniquely one's own. Our collection of interactions with the world, what we make of those interactions, and the exemplars we choose to revere, are a product of our own individual life experience. Our society is not a monolithic entity, especially modern commercial societies. "Our society's values" is actually a rich, diversified, open book, interpreted by each of us in our own way.

Smith writes that as we advance in the "great school of self-command," as we have more practice at viewing ourselves the way others view us, we gradually move from a state of weakness and dependency upon the opinions of others to a state of a little more firmness and independency. A few will reach a state of wisdom in which they need only the approbation of their men within. Such individuals, Smith writes, have "been thoroughly bred in the great school of self-command, in the bustle and business of the world," and have reached a state of "real constancy and firmness" (TMS, 146).

In striving for this state of "real constancy and firmness" Smith compares two different standards of propriety: "The one is the idea of exact propriety and perfection, so far as we are each of us capable of comprehending that idea. The other is that degree of approximation to this idea which is commonly attained in the world..." In the first standard we compare ourselves to some ideal; in the second, we compare ourselves to others in society. This first standard is what the "wise and virtuous man" strives for:

> The wise and virtuous man directs his principal attention
> to the first standard—the idea of exact propriety and per-
> fection. There exists in the mind of every man an idea of
> this kind, gradually formed from his observations upon the
> character and conduct both of himself and of other people.
> It is the slow, gradual, and progressive work of the great
> demigod within the breast, the great judge and arbiter of
> conduct. This idea is in every man more or less accurate-
> ly drawn, its colouring is more or less just, its outlines are
> more or less exactly designed, according to the delicacy
> and acuteness of that sensibility with which those obser-
> vations were made, and according to the care and attention
> employed in making them. (TMS, 247)

Although the "idea of exact propriety" is a result of our observa-

tions of the world, it is a standard we develop all our own, and it necessarily seeks to reach beyond any one of our own circumstantial attachments. When we improve our conduct in some degree, when we take
note that some received wisdom of our upbringing was misleading or
now unfitting, we have made a moral improvement. Smith continues:

> In the wise and virtuous man they [moral improvements]
> have been made with the most acute and delicate sensibil-
> ity, and the utmost care and attention have been employed
> in making them. Every day some feature is improved—
> every day some blemish is corrected. He has studied this
> idea [the idea of exact propriety and perfection] more than
> other people; he comprehends it more distinctly; he has
> formed a much more correct image of it, and is much more
> deeply enamoured of its exquisite and divine beauty: he
> endeavours as well as he can to assimilate his own char-
> acter to this archetype of perfection. But he imitates the
> work of a divine artist, which can never be equalled. (247)

It is important that Smith compares our man within to an artist. Smith perceived a parallel between the process of development
in morals and art. In art, most people in any given generation will
follow the established customs, but, from time-to-time, "an eminent
artist will bring about a considerable change in the established modes
of each of those arts, and introduce a new fashion of writing, music,
or architecture" (TMS, 197). Although these eminent artists inherit certain customs, their development in their respective fields allows
them to make improvements.

While Smith speaks of making keener moral "observations" and
improvements, what I propose to call the moral innovation—analogous to an economic innovation in products or services—is the entire

man within the breast which those improvements and new features belong to. Just as a market innovation, say a new sort of vehicle, will display various new features, a moral innovation, a new sort of conscience, will exhibit various new features.

The man within the breast—or conscience—is the theater of innovation in Smith's moral theory. That is, in Smith's interpretation of the moral sphere, innovations are innovative consciences. In the moral sphere, the adoption by society of one person's innovation is the adoption of that person's conscience. Smith's theorizing accommodated innovation in morals more than is sometimes recognized (DelliSanti forthcoming), just as his theorizing accommodated market innovation and societal dynamism more than is sometimes recognized (DelliSanti 2021).

Smith's account of moral innovation seems to have a distinct Kuhnian flavor: we inherit certain ideas about the world, work within those traditions, but eventually come to realize our own insights. These insights will not be completely unique, since we are always working within a social framework, but they will be wholly new adaptations of old moral insights to new social contexts. Of course, there is no guarantee that everyone will be a major moral innovator, just as there is no guarantee that every scientist will reach a breakthrough, or that every market participant will be an entrepreneur. Smith certainly doesn't believe that everyone will become a "wise and virtuous" man. Most people, most of the time, are more likely to reflect their community's standards than innovate upon them.

But I do think that Smith was aware that the burgeoning commercial age that he was witnessing was going to be a period of great moral innovation—or, perhaps more accurately, a period of great moral tumult. In fact, it already had been. The political and religious turmoil of 17th century England was brought about largely by a population that was increasingly opinionated and individualistic, increasingly interested in defining their own conception of the good life—the "disagreeably rigorous and unsocial" (WN, 796) religious sects that Smith refers to in *Wealth of Nations*. Anna Keay, in *The Restless Republic*, speaks to the climate of 1640s England:

> If the King could be defied, the Archbishop of Canterbury executed and bishops and deans abolished, what else might not be open to question? New notions about society and religion began to germinate, put about and popularized by the printing presses which were now overrun with business. Among the noisiest agitators for change were the London radicals branded 'Levellers' for their egalitarian aspirations. With the distraction of war, and the divisions among the parliamentarians in the 1640s, censorship was patchy and popular debate and discussion reached levels never before seen in England. (Keay 2022, 40)

I think Smith knew the 17th century was not an aberration, that moral tumult would only grow as the division of labor became increasingly complex, commerce brought formerly distant cultures into contact with each other, and more people became enabled to voice their opinions. Indeed, he pessimistically wrote that "[i]n a nation distracted by faction, there are, no doubt, always a few, though commonly but a very few, who preserve their judgment untainted by the general contagion" (TMS, 155).

In "Parmenides Addresses Plato," Jon Murphy and Andrew Humphries (2023) explain the significance of Smith's peculiar tale of Parmenides delivering a philosophical discourse, during which the audience dwindles down until a sole soul remains, namely, Plato. Parmenides is reported by Smith to have said "that Plato alone was audience sufficient for him" (TMS 253). For Smith, one must find some soul to share sentiment with, and hence one is always dependent on social influences. But one may break away from and reject any one social influence, and even a dominant community norm.

Our world has, arguably, grown ever more fragmented and culturally disjointed. Smith does not leave us with a clear theory of how to navigate these strange times, for he too was unsure how to navigate them. However, two elements seem crucial in mitigating the negative side effects of moral innovation, and in benefiting from the positive: (1) humility and (2) an adherence to the liberal plan. To the first suggestion, in *The Wealth of Nations*, Smith recommends "the study of science and philosophy" as well as amusing "publick diversions" as a way of combatting the animosity of hostile factions (WN, 796). By these two mechanisms, members of factions can come to see the extent of their ignorance and gain some epistemic humility.

The second suggestion, adherence to the liberal plan, helps to keep social affairs voluntary and decentralized, and those bottom-up conditions militate against deep moral corruption and large-scale evils (Mueller 2023). Also, the liberal plan militates against using government to impose a vision on the world. Where the rule of law is upheld, where government is chiefly umpire and not a leading player, people will not view it as a tool to force their ideology onto people and crush dissent. Smith's favor for separating church and state reflects his belief that factions are less dangerous where the government neither subsidizes any religion nor restricts the liberty of competing religions.

But, of course, liberal principles are much easier recited than institutionalized. The same spirit of innovation that drives our economy also drives social changes. When everyone is free to try out their own ideas in the marketplace, they are also free to make up their own mind about the truth. And thus, we often find in an otherwise free society contending factions seeking to enlist the government in their schemes to win their political battles and impose their vision of the truth. But I, with Smith, hope that we few, we lonely few, take heart and continue to stand up for and defend good liberal principles in navigating tumultuous times.

References

DelliSanti, Dylan. 2021. The Dynamism of Liberalism: An Esoteric Interpretation of Adam Smith. *Journal of Economic Behavior and Organization* 184: 717–726.

DelliSanti, Dylan. Forthcoming. Moral Innovation and the Man Within the Breast. *Adam Smith Review*, forthcoming.

Fleischacker, Samuel. 2011. Adam Smith and Cultural Relativism. *Erasmus Journal for Philosophy and Economics* 4: 20-41.

Keay, Anna. 2022. *The Restless Republic: Britain without a Crown*. Glasgow: William Collins.

Mueller, Paul D. 2023. Moral Judgment and Governmentalizing Social Affairs. Just Sentiments, March 22.

Murphy, Jon, and Andrew Humphries. 2023. Parmenides Addresses Plato, as Adam Smith Addresses Us. *Just Sentiments*, May 24.

Sen, Amartya. 2009. *The Idea of Justice*. Cambridge: Harvard University Press.

Smith, Adam. 1976 [1776] (WN). *An Inquiry Into the Nature and Causes of The Wealth of Nations*, eds. R. H. Campbell and A. S. Skinner, 2 vols. Oxford: Oxford University Press.

Smith, Adam. 1976 [1790] (TMS). *The Theory of Moral Sentiments*, eds. D. D. Raphael and A.

L. Macfie. Oxford: Oxford University Press.

CHAPTER 19

The Sparing, Indirect, and Invisible Hand: Smith Parries Philo on the Problem of Evil

Paolo Santori

I n his last days, Hume asked Smith to handle the posthumous publication of his *Dialogues Concerning Natural Religion* (DCNR), and Smith refused. Hume died in 1776. DCNR was published in 1779 by arrangements made by his nephew John Home.

In this article, I expound a speculative line of argument to the effect that the first book of *The Wealth of Nations* (WN) can be considered a parry to arguments in DCNR concerning God and the problem of evil.

Max Weber, in "Politics as Vocation," asked, "How could a power that is said to be both omnipotent and good create such an irrational world of unmerited suffering, unpunished justice, and incorrigible stupidity?" (Weber 2004, 86). Weber here summarizes the question of theodicy, namely the relationship between God's justice and worldly evils.

Gottfried Wilhelm von Leibniz coined the term "theodicy" in response to Pierre Bayle's challenge to the Christian belief in divine providence. The debate regarding theodicy has ancient roots but is also widely recognized to have shaped intellectual modernity in Europe (Oslington 2017), when people were more inclined to critically examine God's work. Jacob Viner (1972, 58) said: "Almost every learned Englishman, and still more every learned Scotsman, it would seem, at some stage of his career felt impelled to publish his views on 'The Origin of Evil'." Whether Hume and Smith belong to the modern trend is disputable, yet I pursue a line of thought as though they were speaking to the problem of evil. One clear thing is that otherworldly solutions were neither attractive nor adequate for Hume and Smith.

Hume on idleness and the very sparing hand of nature

At the center of my line of reasoning is the human attribute of idleness and indolence (Santori 2022). Idleness was a central issue for philosophers and theologians in the 17th and 18th centuries. They discussed idleness as an attribute of both the lower classes (poor workers) and upper classes (aristocracy, landlords). But idleness concerns human beings as such, irrespective of social class.

The church fathers and medieval Christianity mostly interpreted idleness and indolence as a manifestation of the sin of sloth, or *Acedia* (Lyman 1989; Sadlek 2004). English and Scottish modernity viewed the concept of idleness through Protestant ethics, which condemned idleness in favor of industriousness as described by Weber (2005, 104). Among the most well-known examples of this attitude is the "Homily Against Idleness," part of the *Books of Homilies*, which, since the 16th century, has been an essential part of the ceremony of the Church of England. Also important was the exhortation of homilies by the Presbyterian-Puritan priest Richard Baxter (Weber 2005). Hume and Smith absorbed the religious atmosphere in the eighteenth century filled with the condemnation of idleness and indolence.

In most of his writings (Schabas and Wennerlind 2008; 2020), Hume discussed the advent of commercial society as an antidote to idleness, as the triumph of industriousness over indolence (Santori 2022). One significant exception is the DCNR. It is known that Hume had been working on it since 1750. When his health deteriorated, Hume appointed Smith to publish his manuscript. In a will drawn up in January 1776, Hume bequeathed to Smith "all [his] manuscripts without exception, desiring him to publish my Dialogues [C]oncerning Natural Religion" (Hume in Rasmussen 2017,188).

The DCNR has three main protagonists. One is the theist *a priori* Demea, who departs the company at the end of Part XI. The other two are the theist *a posteriori* Cleanthes and the skeptic Philo. Whether Cleanthes or Philo best represents Hume's position has long been debated.

Philo treats theodicy. Philo argues that there are four proofs of the non-existence of God, including the God of revealed religions and natural or rational ones. These proofs against God's existence coincide with four worldly evils, each testifying that God's Providence/Nature does not govern our world. The third proof involves idleness.

According to Philo, man is naturally idle or indolent and not inclined to work or put effort into anything. God is responsible for this situation in two respects. On the one hand, though God gave man no special physical advantages to protect himself against hardships of nature, God provided man with reason and sagacity. Second, God made man with a propensity to idleness, which keeps him from achieving his full potential.

Philo says:

> Every animal has the requisite endowments; but these endowments are bestowed with so scrupulous an economy, that any considerable diminution must entirely destroy

the creature .... The human species, **whose chief excellency is reason and sagacity,** is of all the others the most necessitous; and the most deficient in bodily advantages .... An *indulgent parent* would have bestowed a large stock, in order to guard against accidents, and secure the happiness and welfare of the creature, in the most unfortunate concurrence of circumstances. (Hume 2007, 82–83, boldface added)

In order to cure most of the ills of human life, I require not that man should have the wings of the eagle, the swiftness of the stag, the force of the ox, the arms of the lion, the scales of the crocodile or rhinoceros; much less do I demand the sagacity of an angel or cherubim. I am contented to take an increase in one single power or faculty of his soul. **Let him be endowed with a greater propensity to industry and labour; a more vigorous spring and activity of mind; a more constant bent to business and application.** Let the whole species possess naturally an equal diligence with that which many individuals are able to attain by habit and reflection; and **the most beneficial consequences,** without any allay of ill, **is the immediate and necessary result of this endowment.** (Hume 2007, 83, boldface added)

Philo continues his argument,

Almost all the moral, as well as natural evils of human life arise from idleness; and were our species, by the original constitution of their frame, exempt from this vice or infirmity, the perfect cultivation of land, the improvement of arts and manufactures, the exact execution of every office and duty, immediately follow; and men at once may fully reach that state of society, which is so imperfectly attained by the best regulated government. But as industry is a power, and the most valuable of any, nature seems determined, suitably to her usual maxims, to bestow it on men with **a very sparing hand**; and rather to punish him severely for his deficiency in it, than to reward him for his attainments. She has so contrived his frame, that nothing but the most violent necessity can oblige him to labour; **and she employs all his other wants to overcome**, at least in part, **the want of diligence, and to endow him with some share of a faculty,** of which she has thought fit naturally to bereave him. (Hume 2007, 83–84, boldface added)

The "very sparing hand" of Nature/God provided human beings, whose excellence lies in "reason and sagacity," with little or no propensity to "industry and labour." All human evils derive from this shortage. Philo's hyperbolic tone could have been pedagogical, to warn against the risks of indolence (Matson 2021).

Thus, Philo advanced a social and economic argument against the existence and justice of God. It is also true that Philo saw an opening for hope in Nature's work because it employs other human desires "to overcome, at least in part, the want of diligence." We may think of Smith as taking this opening to defend God's Providence. The good functioning of commercial society is Smith's theodicy, a parry to Philo's argument.

Hume uses "very sparing hand" to describe the operation of nature. Perhaps we meet here one more source of Smith's invisible hand to add to the ones in the literature. I believe that Smith was not convinced by the atheistic conclusion reached in Part XI of DCNR, even though in the next and final Part, Philo seems closer to the cautious theism of Cleanthes. We know that Hume refused to identify as an atheist, feeling the skeptic category more appropriate (Coleman in Hume 2007, xxxix n31). Nonetheless, in Part XI the core of Philo's provocation about theodicy remained unchallenged.

Smith's parry: *The Wealth of Nations*

In WN, in the second chapter, Smith mentions human beings' "propensity to truck, barter, and exchange" (25). Behind this propensity is "[t]he uniform, constant, and uninterrupted effort of every man to better his condition" (WN 343). These propensities produce the division of labor that, in turn, causes "[t]he greatest improvement in the productive powers of labour, and the greater part of the skill, dexterity, and judgment with which it is anywhere directed, or applied" (WN 13). They impel man to help others since only then will they help him. Man is naturally concerned for his familiars, but he is also impelled to address strangers cooperatively, with a "regard to their own interest" (WN 27). The public good is thereby advanced.

After introducing "the propensity to truck, barter, and exchange," Smith adds: "Whether this propensity be one of those original principles in human nature, of which no further account can be given; or whether, as seems more probable, it be the necessary consequence of the faculties of reason and speech, it belongs not to our present subject to enquire" (WN 25). The "disposition of trucking" was in Smith's lessons of 1762–1763, after, as Dennis Rasmussen suggests (2017, 187), Smith was likely to have read Hume's DCNR. As recorded in *Lectures on Jurisprudence*, Smith said: "If we should inquire into the principle in the human mind on which this disposition of trucking is founded, it is clearly the natural inclination every one has to persuade" (LJ 352). These passages from WN and LJ closely resemble the "reason and sagacity" mentioned by Philo. Smith's argument about propensities might be seen as an answer to the theodicy problem, parrying Philo's atheistic argument.

In both DCNR and WN, human beings are described as needing the services of fellow citizens. Benevolence is insufficient for human beings to care for one another. The missing ingredient in Philo's argument, the propensities to better one's conditions and exchange, emerges at this point. Smith writes:

> And thus the certainty of being able to exchange all that surplus part of the produce of his own labour ... encourages every man to apply himself to a particular occupation, and to cultivate and bring to perfection whatever talent or genius he may possess for that particular species of business. (WN 28)

Similar reasoning is found in Smith's LJ: "The offering of a shilling, which to us appears to have so plain and simple a meaning, is in reality offering an argument to persuade one to do so and so as it is for his interest" (352).

Smith concedes that God/Nature did not directly bequeath man with the propensity to work hard and reject idleness. But human beings are created with propensities that put in communication their different interests and, in so doing, arouse their motivation to work. As far as the butcher, the baker and the brewer are concerned, "[w]e address ourselves, not to their humanity but to their self-love, and never talk to them of our own necessities but of their advantages" (WN 27). The "evil" of human idleness is defeated by the combination of propensities to improve and exchange. Again, Philo's third argument about evil proving God's inexistence is parried.

The sparing, invisible hand

Philo said that if only man had been endowed with a natural love of being industrious, "the most beneficial consequences, without any allay of ill, is the immediate and necessary result" (Hume 2007, 83). In the DCNR (2007, 83), Hume cited "the perfect cultivation of land," "the improvement of the arts" and the "exact execution of every office and duty." To sum up, Philo says, "men at once may fully reach that state of society, which is so imperfectly attained by the best regulated government" (2007, 83-84). Suppose one approaches the first book of WN through this lens. In that case, it is impossible not to apprehend a demonstration of how beneficial consequences like those listed by Hume arise from the propensities toward betterment and exchange. The operations of natural forces implanted by God means that his hand is not "sparing." The invisible hand of God only seems sparing because God's creation, Nature (including human nature), operates indirectly. The direct approach would have been for God to make man to love being industrious. Instead, God made man to love things that become gettable by being industrious.

The introduction and first two chapters of book one of WN clearly lay out the indirectness. First, Smith affirms that "[t]he annual labour of every nation is the fund which originally supplies it with all the necessaries and conveniences of life" and that, in this respect, "the skill, dexterity, and judgment with which its labour is generally applied" plays a decisive role (WN 10). Smith remarks that "the greater part of the skill, dexterity, and judgment" of humankind is the effect of the division of labour (WN 13). To conclude the argument, he envisages the division of labour as the natural and gradual consequence of "the propensity to truck, barter, and exchange" interacting with man's urge to improvement (WN 25). The additional elements of the limit of commercial society, the role of the state in regulating markets and the role of man's self-command or deserved esteem do not refute Smith's central message in WN. Smith's best arguments to defend God's work against the charge raised by Philo's consideration of human evil are thus the birth of commercial society and the opulence of markets to the private and public good.

Why would God opt for the indirect approach?

Thus, we might see Smith as suggesting that God's hand is not only invisible but sparing and indirect. As a matter of God's designs, one might still ask: Why would God choose such an indirect approach rather than a more direct one as Philo proposed, whether it be simply supplying man's wants in abundance or endowing man with a love of industry.

Those are the sorts of questions one gets into when one tries to fathom God's design. Here Philo's skepticism may be apt:

> All that belongs to human understanding, in this deep ignorance and obscurity, is to be sceptical, or at least cautious; and not to admit of any hypothesis, whatever; much less, of any which is supported by no appearance of probability. Now this **I assert to be the case with regard to all the causes of evil, and the circumstances, on which it depends"** (Hume 2007, 80, boldface added).

References

Hume, David. 1888. *Letters of David Hume to William Strahan*. Oxford: Clarendon Press.

Hume, David. 2007. *Hume: Dialogues Concerning Natural Religion: And Other Writings*, ed. Dorothy Coleman. Cambridge: Cambridge University Press.

Lyman, Stanford M. 1989. *The Seven Deadly Sins: Society and Evil*. Lanham: Rowman & Littlefield Publishers.

Matson, Erik W. 2021. A Dialectical Reading of Adam Smith on Wealth and Happiness. *Journal of Economic Behavior & Organization* 184: 826-836.

Oslington, Paul. 2017. *Political Economy as Natural Theology: Smith, Malthus and Their Followers*. London: Routledge.

Rasmussen, Dennis C. 2017. *The Infidel and the Professor: David Hume, Adam Smith, and the Friendship that Shaped Modern Thought*. Princeton and Oxford: Princeton University Press.

Sadlek, Gregory M. 2004. *Idleness Working: The Discourse of Love's Labor from Ovid through Chaucer and Gower*. Washington, D.C.: CUA Press.

Santori, Paolo. 2022. Idleness and the Very Sparing Hand of God: The Invisible Tie between Hume's Dialogues Concerning Natural Religion and Smith's Wealth of Nations. *Journal of the History of Economic Thought* 44(2): 246-267.

Smith, Adam. 1978. *Lectures on Jurisprudence*. Vol. 5. VM eBooks.

Smith, Adam. 1981. *An Inquiry into the Nature and Causes of the Wealth of Nations*. Vol 1. Indianapolis: Liberty Fund.

Schabas, Margaret, and Carl Wennerlind. 2008. *David Hume's Political Economy*. London and New York: Routledge.

Schabas, Margaret, and Carl Wennerlind. 2020. *A Philosopher's Economist: David Hume and the Rise of Capitalism*. Chicago: University of Chicago Press.

Viner, Jacob. 1972. *The Role of Providence in the Social Order: An Essay in Intellectual History*. Princeton: Princeton University Press.

Waterman, A. M. C. 2017. *Revolution, Economics and Religion*. London: Routledge.

Weber, Max. [1904–1905] 2005. *The Protestant Ethic and the Spirit of Capitalism*. London and New York: Routledge.

Weber, Max. 2004. *The Vocation Lectures*, eds. David Owen and Tracy B. Strong. Indianapolis: Hackett Publishing.

Weber, Max. 2009. *From Max Weber; Essays in Sociology*, eds. H. H. Gerth and C. Wright Mills. London and New York: Routledge.

CHAPTER 20

Between the Lines of Adam Smith's Endorsement of an Interest-rate Cap

Jonathon Diesel

Almost all of what Adam Smith says about loans and interest would lead you to believe that he sees it as an integral piece of the free-enterprise system. Just as Smith dispelled confusions about the demand and supply of gold and silver, likening them to the supply and demand of "pots and pans" (WN, 439), Smith sees the demand and supply of loanable funds as like rental markets for other resources. At the start of the chapter "Of Stock Lent at Interest" in the *Wealth of Nations*, Smith says that interest is "annual rent for the use of it [stock]" (350).

Odd, then, is the endorsement that Smith—the apostle of "allowing every man to pursue his own interest his own way"—gives to the status-quo cap on interest rates. Jeremy Bentham in 1787 famously and incisively upbraided Smith for the flagrant departure from his own teachings.

Smith does not propose caps on other rental rates or indeed any other kind of prices. So why this one?

Also odd is Smith's argumentation for the cap. Whatever sense we try to make of Smith's argumentation, it can be subverted by the logic of his own immediately subsequent remarks.

Things become odder still in view of what Smith said elsewhere about caps on interest rates—and in view of what he *did not say* elsewhere (for example in the public-policy portion of his *Lectures on Jurisprudence*).

I suggest that Smith's endorsement was not wholehearted, even that it was dissembling. The present piece is based on a dissertation chapter, subsequently published in *Journal of Economic Behavior and Organization*, "Adam Smith on Usury: An Esoteric Reading"). Here I avoid extensive analysis of Smith's text, the discourse situation at Smith's time, and subsequent scholarship, instead making the main points for an esoteric reading.

Peak esotericism

The time in which Smith lived was a time of peak esotericism, as explained by Arthur Melzer in his master work on esoteric writing and its role in history (Melzer 2014, 12–29, 96). Signs of esoteric writing in a text, Melzer notes, include "something [that] jars the reader, such as incongruity or an uncharacteristic misquotation, it can serve as a marker for where an author has hidden his or her true meaning" (p. 296). Melzer quotes Alexander Pope:

> *Those oft are stratagems which errors seem*
> *Nor is it Homer nods, but we that dream.*

Melzer explains that an author may also hide his true message by dispersing it piecemeal throughout his work (p. 317), and that too pertains to our issue here with Smith.

Dugald Stewart (1753–1828) was well acquainted with Smith,

personally and intellectually. He led the way on our issue. Stewart insinuated that Smith dissembled on interest-rate caps, in both *Account of the Life and Writings of Adam Smith* ([1795]) and *Lectures on Political Economy* ([1856]). Stewart follows Jeremy Bentham in rejecting Smith's position on interest-rate caps. Stewart plays a deft game of association where he likens Smith's tepid justification to that of John Locke's on the same topic. Stewart goes on to point out that most of Locke's positions were quite liberal in nature, and that his justification for regulating interest rates were likely an appeasement of current conventions and a compromise of principle to mollify readers (Stewart [1795], 349). Stewart is explicit that Locke dissembled and created the association, strongly suggesting that Smith did as well (Diesel 2021, 734).

In Smith's writings we find abundant instances of slyness or esotericism. Smith himself taught his students about tactful engagement (LRBL 111-5, 146-7). David Hume's experience taught valuable lessons about being too direct (Diesel 2021, 736). The Frenchman Pierre-Samuel Dupont de Nemours wrote to Smith in 1788, explaining that in his own work he tempers things: "By assaulting their eyes with a bright light, we would reconstitute their blindness" (quoted in Prasch and Warin 2009, 69). Dupont would later use the same blinding-light metaphor in suggesting that Smith himself engaged in the same sort of dissembling (Dupont [1809], 179).

But why be esoteric about interest-rate caps? Here are some broad points that might begin to answer the question:

- The concept of usury had a long religious and Biblical tradition behind it, a tradition that promulgated interest-rate restrictions throughout much of the world and over centuries. Smith may have been reluctant to deploy free-market economics to attack laws with strong religious overtones. Libertarians today who favor the freedom to sell sex do not necessarily lead with that unseemly point. Likewise, one might have been reluctant to advocate the freedom to charge 'usurious' interest rates. Let me add that in researching the intellectual history of usury, I have come to believe that Smith is not unique; many economic writers, including theologians, treated the topic in ways that seem like dissembling.

- Smith's goal was to persuade the aristocracy to embrace liberalism. Such a hope might be dashed by too bold a proclamation. Perhaps it is best to take Smith's advice regarding Solon, and when the ideal is too much to bear seek the compromise that moves things in the right direction (TMS 233; Clark 2021).

- Perhaps Smith was worried that an outright endorsement of unregulated loans would appear too friendly to the growing merchant class.

- Smith may have figured that he would leave it to some forward soul like Bentham to point out the flimsiness of his reasoning and to advocate the legalization of usury. Here it is important to note that justification that Smith gives for the cap does *not* invoke the traditional grounds of protecting the poor from exploitative lenders; by shifting the grounds of the justification to economic production, Smith paves the way for someone like Bentham to correct his faulty argumentation.

What Smith says

In the discussion of interest-rate controls that leads to his endorsement of the cap, Smith begins by describing the worst-case scenario of outright bans on interest. No one will lend money without interest. Smith understands that black markets and exploitation are the result of prohibition:

> In some countries the interest of money has been prohibited by law... This regulation, instead of preventing, has been found from experience to increase the evil of usury; the debtor being obliged to pay, not only for the use of the money, but for the risk which his creditor runs by accepting a compensation for that use. He is obliged, if one may say so, to insure his creditor from the penalties of usury. (WN 356)

Next he says that if the cap is fixed too low, "the effects of this fixation must be nearly the same as those of a total prohibition of interest." Smith continues: "If it is fixed precisely at the lowest market price, it ruins with honest people, who respect the laws of their country, the credit of all those who cannot give the very best security, and obliges them to have recourse to exorbitant usurers [in black markets, that is]."

It is then that Smith endorses the status-quo cap: "In a country, such as Great Britain, where money is lent to government at three per cent. and to private people upon good security at four, and four and a half, *the present legal rate, five per cent., is perhaps, as proper as any*" (WN 356-7; italics added). And he begins the next paragraph by reiterating that endorsement: "The legal rate [that is, the cap], it is to be observed, though it ought to be somewhat above, ought not to be much above the lowest market rate."

Smith follows immediately with his justification for such a cap, called "the legal rate," as opposed to a higher cap:

If the legal rate of interest in Great Britain, for example, was fixed so high as eight or ten per cent., the greater part of the money which was to be lent, would be lent to prodigals and projectors, who alone would be willing to give this high interest. Sober people, who will give for the use of money no more than a part of what they are likely to make by the use of it, would not venture into the competition. A great part of the capital of the country would thus be kept out of the hands which were most likely to make a profitable and advantageous use of it, and thrown into those which were most likely to waste and destroy it. (WN, 357.15)

Smith does not explain why, in a freer market, lenders would tend to lend to unsober borrowers. One might infer that Smith is implying that lenders are fated to blindness about the soberness of borrowers, and thus, from the lenders' perspective, the market for borrowers is like the "market for lemons" in a famous but fantastically far-fetched model (Akerlof 1970).

But what directly follows subverts that reading of Smith, for Smith writes:

Where the legal rate of interest, on the contrary, is fixed but a very little above the lowest market rate, **sober people are universally preferred, as borrowers, to prodigals and projectors.** The person who lends money gets nearly as much interest from the former as he dares to take from the latter, and his money is much safer in the hands of the one set of people, than in those of the other. A great part of the capital of the country is thus thrown into the hands in which it is most likely to be employed with advantage. (357, boldface added)

So Smith believes that lenders can distinguish the sober from the unsober. Indeed, and as Stewart had noted about Smith's texts, Smith himself said that most lenders are judicious and borrowers circumspect (WN 342, 350).

What's more, just a few lines after saying that lenders can distinguish between the sober and unsober, Smith speaks of the experience in France when the king attempted to reduce the cap from five to four percent: "money continued to be lent in France at five per cent., the law being evaded in several different ways" (358).

Some commentators have neglected Smith's statement about the ability of lenders to distinguish sober and unsober and, on that basis, relate Smith's discussion to models of asymmetric information in a credit-rationing framework (Stiglitz and Weiss 1981; see Hollander 1999, 528, 544-5). But even if you give Smith only that careless reading, it still would not work as justification for the government imposition of a cap, because, in a free-market lenders could of their own choosing refrain from lending at high rates, simply to attract some of the sober borrowers to their pool of applicants.

Bentham's *Defence of Usury* (1787) takes Smith to task. The work was very influential in setting the tone on lending headed into the modern era (Houkes 2004, 394; Persky 2007, 234-5; Rockoff 2009, 295; Chesterton 1933, 67). The 13th letter is specifically addressed to Smith, and it does a convincing job of using Smith's own words against him on the matter—although Bentham failed to use Smith's own admission that lenders can distinguish the sober from the unsober.

There is anecdotal evidence from a personal engagement about what Smith said to his visitor when asked about Bentham's critique. The report is consistent with the idea that Smith's heart was not really in the endorsement he had given to the status-quo cap on interest rates (see Rae 1895, 423-24; Pesciarelli 1989, 532; Viner 1965, 19; Paganelli 2003, 45).

References

Akerlof, George A. 1970. The Market for 'Lemons': Quality Uncertainty and the Market Mechanism. *Quarterly Journal of Economics* 84(3): 488–500.

Bentham, Jeremy. 1818 [1787]. *Defence of Usury*. Library of Economics and Liberty.

Chesterton, Gilbert K. 1933. *St. Thomas Aquinas*. New York: Sheed & Ward.

Clark, Michael J. 2021. Adam Smith as Solon: Accommodating on the Edges of Liberty, Not Abandoning It. *Journal of Economic Behavior and Organization* 184: 739–747.

Condillac, Abbé de. 2008 [1776]. *Commerce and Government Considered in Their Mutual Relationship*, trans. Shelagh Eltis. Indianapolis: Liberty Fund.

Diesel, Jonathon. 2021. Adam Smith on Usury: An Esoteric Reading. *Journal of Economic Behavior & Organization* 184: 727-738.

Dupont de Nemours, Pierre-Samuel. 2011 [1809]. Remarks from 1809 by Dupont de Nemours on Adam Smith. Translated by Frederick Sautet. *Econ Journal Watch* 8(2): 174-184.

Hollander, Samuel. 1973. *The Economics of Adam Smith*. Toronto: University of Toronto Press.

Hollander, Samuel. 1999. Jeremy Bentham and Adam Smith on the Usury Laws: A 'Smithian' Reply to Bentham and a New Problem. *European Journal of the History of Economic Thought* (4): 523-551.

Houkes, John M. 2004. *An Annotated Bibliography on the History of Usury and Interest From the Earliest Times Through the Eighteenth Century*. New York: Edwin Mellen Press.

Melzer, Arthur M. 2014. *Philosophy Between the Lines: The Lost History of Esoteric Writing*. Chicago: University of Chicago Press.

Paganelli, Maria Pia. 2003. In Medio Stat Virtus: An Alternative View of Usury in Adam Smith's Thinking. *History of Political Economy* 35 (1): 21-48.

Pesciarelli, Enzo. 1989. Smith, Bentham, and the Development of Contrasting Ideas on Entrepreneurship. *History of Political Economy* 21(3).

Persky, Joseph. 2007. Retrospectives: From Usury to Interest. *Journal of Economic Perspectives* 21(1): 227-236.

Prasch, Robert, and Thierry Warin. 2009. 'Il est encore plus important de bien faire que de bien dire': A Translation and Analysis of Dupont de Nemours' 1788 Letter to Adam Smith. *History of Economics Review* 49: 67-75.

Rae, John. 1895. *Life of Adam Smith*. London: Macmillan and Co.

Rockoff, Hugh. 2009. Prodigals and Projectors: An Economic History of Usury Laws in the United States from Colonial Times to 1900. In *Human Capital and Institutions: A Long Run View*. Edited by David Eltis, Frank D. Lewis, and Kenneth L. Sokoloff. New York: Cambridge University.

Smith, Adam. 1981 [1776]. *An Inquiry into the Nature and Causes of the Wealth of Nations*, eds. R.H. Campbell and A.S. Skinner. Indianapolis: Liberty Fund.

Smith, Adam. 1982 [1759]. *The Theory of Moral Sentiments*, eds. D.D. Raphael and A.L. Macfie. Indianapolis: Liberty Fund.

Smith, Adam. 1985 [1983]. *Lectures on Rhetoric and Belles Lettres*, ed. J.C. Bryce. Indiana: Liberty Fund.

Smith, Adam. 1987 [1977]. *Correspondence of Adam Smith*. Edited by E.C. Mossner and I.S. Ross. Indiana: Liberty Fund.

Stewart, Dugald. 1971 [1856]. *The Collected Works of Dugald Stewart: Volume IX. Westmead*, England: Gregg International Publishers.

Stewart, Dugald.1982 [1795] An Account of the Life and Writings of Adam Smith, LL.D. *Essays on Philosophical Subjects*. Indianapolis: Liberty Fund.

Stiglitz, Joseph E., and Andrew Weiss. 1981. Credit Rationing in Markets with Imperfect Information. *American Economic Review* 71(3): 393-410.

Viner, Jacob. 1965. *Guide to John Rae's Life of Adam Smith*. New York: Kelley.

CHAPTER 21

Bridging Cultures: Adam Smith and Confucius

Hairuo Tan

Different cultural perspectives sometimes clash, but universal truths can transcend cultural barriers. Adam Smith theorized from a belief in a universal human nature that spans culture, history, and nation. He levelled distinctions commonly made in his day between the nature of street porters and philosophers, rich and poor, and enslaved and free. He described Europeans and Chinese as "brethren" (TMS 136.4).

If Smith had been able to converse across the centuries with Confucius, they might have found much to appreciate in one another's ideas. There is in fact common ground between their views on interpersonal relations, propriety, and the cultivation of moral values (Tan, forthcoming). It seems possible that each would perceive the other man's perspectives as complementary to his own.

Smith did not own copies of Confucius's work. He possibly was aware of Confucius's ideas, although this cannot be definitively established. There were during Smith's lifetime translations of Confucius's *Analects* of which he would have been aware. The first translation of *The Analects* into European languages was published in 1687 in Latin. This translation formed the basis of all later French and English translations available during Smith's lifetime (St André 2018, 229). Robert Molesworth, who personally knew and influenced Smith's teacher Francis Hutcheson, seems to have read Confucius. He recommended Confucius in correspondence with William Wishart, who served as principal of Edinburgh University from 1736 to 1753 (Rivers 2000, 176).

Imagine a conversation between Smith and Confucius on moral philosophy. Smith initiates the discussion with his theory of sympathy. He introduces the spectator-agent relation. Moral judgment requires a spectator to inhabit the agent's situation. He must become "in some measure the same person" as the agent to perceive how the agent is affected and to form a proper judgment (TMS 9.2).

Confucius might respond with his theory of *shu*, a concept analogous to sympathy in function and importance. Shu "can serve as a guide for one's entire life"; it is a sense of likeness between human beings (Analects, 15.24). Confucius would elucidate the moral implications of shu: "Do not impose upon others what you yourself do not desire" (Analects 12.2 and 15.24), which implicitly suggests the practice of transposition. One should expect what he himself does not favor is unlikely to be favored by another. As commented by E. G. Slingerland, a translator of *The Analects*, "The fact that you yourself hate hunger and cold allows you to understand that everyone in the world desires food and clothing" (p. 183). The corollary is that an individual ought to help others secure what she herself desires. Confucius taught his disciples that: "Desiring to take his stand, one ... helps others to take their stands. Wanting to realize himself, he helps others to realize themselves" (Analects, 6.30). One guided by the doctrine of shu would initiate an action impacting others, only when he could appreciate the impact of this proposed action if he himself were made the bearer of this action.

Smith might point out that Confucius's account of moral judgment thus far presented crucially lacks an intermediary figure comparable to his impartial spectator, a concept introduced in his own work in the discussion of "noble and generous resentment" (TMS 24.4). Resentment becomes noble and generous only when an impartial spectator approves of the indignation. One's endeavor in moderating her passion to a pitch that the impartial spectator would approve of will gain her the sympathy of any ordinary spectator who consults the impartial spectator. Proper moral judgment requires a third person perspective.

Confucius would rejoin by noting that a sense of impartiality is inherent, albeit implicit, in *shu*, which implies "listening to the hearts of the other" (Wu 2013, 433).

As the conversation moved forward, both men would find themselves discussing individuals' sociability and the common good. Human beings are not isolated islands; they naturally are embedded and active in social life, Smith would say. When conflicts of interests arise during a social interaction, one's private interest should be advanced only on the supposition that if another were to do likewise, the interests of the community, country, and even universe would advance (TMS 235.3).

Confucius would concur, perhaps recalling a situation in which he criticized two of his disciples for failing to dissuade their master from initiating an unjust war. These disciples erred by failing to reconcile their personal interests and the interests of their master with the higher good, which is the preservation of harmony and peace among different municipality states (Analects 16.1).

The conversation between Confucius and Smith would inevitably touch on considerations of the supreme good. Is there an authoritative standard of the good above the authority of any human judge? Smith would argue that one's faculty of judgment is flows from "[t]he all-wise Author of Nature" (TMS 128.31). Above the "immediate judgment of mankind" exists a higher tribunal of "the supposed impartial spectator" (TMS 130.32). And above this higher tribunal exits "a still higher tribunal," where is seated "the all-seeing Judge of the world, whose eye can never be deceived, and whose judgments can never be perverted" (TMS 131.33). Smith thus acknowledges a supreme judge endowed with superhuman authority.

Confucius would likely refrain from rejecting such a judge. But he would not feel confident in elaborating further. Confucius held spiritual forces in deep reverence (Analects 6.22), although he believed them to be fundamentally incomprehensible (Analects 11.12). He did not teach his disciples anything that he himself could not comprehend, but he believed in judgments made from the above. Even during his travels among municipality states, when he struggled to have his teachings recognized by their leaders, he maintained the belief that tian (heaven) would recognize his efforts (Analects 14.35). On another occasion, when one of his disciples expressed dissatisfaction with his meeting with a woman of questionable reputation, Confucius swore an oath, willing to accept punishment from tian if he had acted inappropriately (Analects 6.28).

While Smith was influenced by Christian writings, and Confucius lived in a time when there was a lack of systematically written theological works, and spiritual forces were often associated with mythological tales, these differing lifetime experiences did not prevent them from finding common ground in acknowledging a supreme judge.

As their conversation evolved, the topic of rules of propriety would come into focus. Smith would argue that propriety is by nature at least somewhat "loose, vague, and indeterminate" (TMS 327.1). Unlike a grammar book that defines rules rather exactly, propriety depends on moral judgments of a less exact nature. The "suitableness or unsuitableness" of a sentiment concerning a particular cause determines the propriety or impropriety of an action (TMS 18.6). A spectator continuously assesses an agent's behavior, but not only that—the spectator also evaluates his own judgments. Furthermore, each judgment is enriched by past judgments (Matson et al. 2019). Rules of propriety are dynamic and subject to how the spectator adapts his judgments.

Smithian propriety finds a counterpart in Confucius's treatment of *li* (ritual propriety). Despite its literal translation, which suggests a grammar-like sense, *li* possesses elements of recursiveness, adjustment, and spontaneity. Confucius famously advocated "to return to *li*" (Analects 12.1), but this wasn't a call for a rigid return to the past. Adhering to *li* involves more an internal moral improvement than an external adherence to fixed rituals. What is considered "abiding by *li*" today might be seen as "against *li*" tomorrow. One who refuses to update his perception on *li* will eventually fail to act as *li* requires.

Confucianism, the philosophical tradition which borrowed the name of Confucius, failed to transmit the heritage of Confucius in its originality. One significant departure from Confucius's teaching is the diminishing emphasis of the dynamism in *li*. When the influence of Confucianism peaked in Imperial China, *li*, instead of guiding individual's moral improvement, it became an instrument employed by authoritarian rulers to regulate the external conduct and suppress the internal mindset of their subjects. Mistaking Confucianism for Confucius's teachings can make Confucius antagonistic to the classical liberal tradition. Studying Confucius's own words unmolested by any self-declared admirers of Confucius overcomes this artificially made conflict.

Smith might utilize his description of the prudent man (TMS 213–217), emphasizing the role of prudence in fostering habits of industry, steadiness, and moderation, while alleviating the anxiety, busyness, and restlessness that stem from the love of praise (Hanley 2009, 103). A prudent man is an industrious learner, driven by a genuine desire "to understand whatever he professes to understand, and not merely to persuade other people that he understands" (TMS 213.7). Confucius would say that he too believed in the central importance of prudence, pointing out his teaching on the pleasure of studying and practicing what has been learned at the right time (Analects 1.1). Confucius considered himself a lifelong learner, and never discriminated when choosing his teacher. He was ready to emulate any passer-by in whom he could find merits (Analects 7.22). Confucius might also supplement with his account of avoiding the love of praise. Confucius once reminded his disciples that they should not be worried about how their abilities were recognized by others but should be more concerned whether they paid enough respect to others' abilities (Analects 1.16).

Smith would emphasize another trait of the prudent man: the avoidance of factions or cliques. A prudent man connects himself with little clubs or cabals only when compelled by self-defense (TMS 213-214.7). Confucius would appreciate this quality, as he taught the importance of seeking harmony with neighbors without seeking their favor by trying to become like them (Analects 13.23). Smith might add that when one discusses a topic of his expertise, one cannot expect his audience to share the same familiarity or fascination with it, necessitating a degree of reserve and avoiding excessive enthusiasm (TMS 33-34.6). Confucius would consider reserve not only a matter of expediency but a virtue to be cultivated. He stressed the importance of careful speech, advocating that one should be slow to speak but quick to act and should feel shame if his conduct does not align with his words (Analects 4.24). Additionally, Confucius would suggest that reserve can sometimes provide protection. This concern is likely rooted in the turbulent time he lived in. Confucius taught that when a state is governed along the wrong path, one's speech should be conciliatory (Analects 14.3). In other words, one is not expected to challenge the authorities with audacious criticism.

Another noteworthy characteristic of a prudent man likely to find resonance with Confucius is that, as Smith says, a prudent man "confines himself, as much as his duty will permit, to his own affairs" (TMS 215.13). Such confining should not be interpreted as selfishness, but as a prudent man's awareness of what the society demands of him. Confucius would likely express a similar viewpoint, particularly with an emphasis on political affairs. He advised: "Do not discuss matters of government policy that do not fall within the scope of your official duties" (Analects 8.14 and 14.26). Not holding a government position, Confucius refrained from providing advice on policy matters. This shared perspective emphasizes the importance of recognizing one's role and responsibilities within the broader social context.

Smith and Confucius could further exchange their thoughts on self-command. According to Smith, passions that need to be commanded can be placed into two classes. The first class includes fear and anger, and the second class love of ease, pleasure, and applause, and of many other selfish gratifications (TMS 238.3). Confucius, in response, would highlight the valor of an individual who is not driven by fear (Analects 9.29) and would acknowledge what Smith wrote about the valor of "[t]he heroes of ancient and modern history, who... have perished upon the scaffold, and who behaved there with ease and dignity" (TMS 238.5). Smith would then share the story of the poor man's son. The poor man's son sees that the rich and the great people have more means of happiness, and thus he strives to become rich. He forgoes "the humble security and contentment," only to find himself in no better situation, since "wealth and greatness are mere trinkets of frivolous utility" (TMS 181.8). True happiness, according to Smith, consists in tranquility and enjoyment: "Without tranquillity there can be no enjoyment" (TMS 149.30). The poor man's son's pursuit of wealth and greatness can merely bring him the "pleasure of vanity and superiority," which are "seldom consistent with perfect tranquillity" (TMS 150.31).

In response, Confucius might recount the story of his disciple Yan Hui, whom Confucius praised for his unwavering moral character. Living a simple life with only a humble bowl of food and a modest place to rest, Yan Hui's joy remains undisturbed (Analects 6.11). Smith may recognize in Yan Hui a resemblance to the philosopher-beggar, "who suns himself by the side of the highway [yet] possesses that security which kings are fighting for" (TMS 158.10). This exchange of stories would underscore the shared perspectives on the importance of self-command and the true sources of happiness.

At the end of their conversation, Confucius might reflect on the supreme objective of his teaching, guiding his disciples to become more like a *junzi*, an exemplary person who is capable of all virtues and is perfect in morality. Social status, occupation, and upbringing are all rendered inessential in the pursuit of becoming a *junzi*. Confucius himself was always ready to bring knowledge to anyone seeking education. What truly matters is what resides in one's heart and his dedication to constant self-reflection and moral cultivation. The moral improvement and virtues discussed throughout this hypothetical conversation all contribute to the qualities of a *junzi*, but are insufficient to make one a junzi, as a *junzi* is an ideal too perfect to find in real life.

Here I have offered several comparisons between Smith and Confucius. The chief comparisons are presented in the following figure:

	Adam Smith	Confucius
The theory of sympathy	Transposition	
	Impartial spectator	shu «恕» (reciprocity)
The supreme judge	The existence of a power above humankind	
	"the all-seeing Judge of the world, whose eye can never be deceived, and whose judgements can never be perverted" (TMS 131.33)	"While you are not able to serve men, how could you be able to serve the spirit?" (Analects 11.12) tian «天» (bearer of supreme power)
The theory of propriety	"Loose, vague, and indeterminate" (TMS III.6.11)	
	"suitableness or unsuitableness» of the sentiment with respect to the cause" (TMS 18.6) The ladder of propriety (Matson et al, 2019)	"Conquer your self and return to li «礼» (ritual) ..." (Analects 12.1) The recursiveness of li
Virtues	A person of exemplary or ideal conduct	
	"The wise and virtuous man" (TMS 247.25)	A junzi «君子» (gentleman) is ren «仁».

Having proposed an imaginary conversation between two great thinkers of different times and cultures—Smith as an indispensable contributor of the Western liberal tradition and Confucius as a crucial mind of ancient Chinese civilization—this article hopes to provoke further explorations on cross-cultural communications. Finding the universal truth in a culture that seems quite different from one's own does not homogenize the two cultures, but it may harmonize them. It helps to harmonize the diversity of human cultures. Different civilizations may then live in greater harmony, and peace. To strive to truthfully consult Smith's impartial spectator or to behave more prox-imately to the standards as required by Confucius's junzi will not cre-ate two sets of human beings with an identical mindset. But those determined to pursue either track will likely find their counterpart pursuing the other track to be praiseworthy.

References:

Confucius. 2003. *Confucius Analects: With Selections from Traditional Commentaries,* trans. Edward Gilman Slingerland. Indianapolis, IN: Hackett Publishing Company Incorporated.

Hanley, Ryan Patrick. 2009. *Adam Smith and the Character of Virtue.* Cambridge, UK: Cambridge University Press.

Matson, Erik W., Colin Doran, and Daniel B. Klein. 2019. "Hume and Smith on Utili-ty, Agreeableness, Propriety, and Moral Approval." *History of European Ideas* 45(5): 675-704. London: Routledge.

Rivers, Isabel. 2000. *Reason, Grace, and Sentiment: Volume 2, Shaftesbury to Hume: A Study of the Language of Religion and Ethics in England,* 1660–1780. Cambridge, UK: Cambridge University Press.

Smith, Adam. 1982. *The Theory of Moral Sentiments.* Edited by Raphael and Macfie. Indianapolis, IN: Liberty Fund.

St André, James. 2018. *Translating China as Cross-Identity Performance.* Honolulu, HI: University of Hawaii Press.

Tan, Hairuo. Forthcoming. Adam Smith and Confucius on Morality: A Comparative Study of *The Theory of Moral Sentiments and The Analects of Confucius. In The Adam Smith Review: Vol. 14,* ed. Fonna Forman. London: Routledge.

Wu, Meiyao. 2013. "Ren-Li, Reciprocity, Judgment, and the Question of Openness to the Other in the Confucian Lunyu." *Journal of Moral Education* 42(4): 430–42.

CHAPTER 22

Adam Smith on Education Funding

Scott Drylie

In the *Wealth of Nations* (WN), Adam Smith dedicates a long chapter to examining the merits of government expenses. In that chapter he includes an article which has attracted considerable attention: "Of the Expence of the Institutions for the Education of Youth." This article is the primary place in which he addresses the education of youth—those years from elementary through college and university (the latter starting several years earlier than they do today).

Since the Progressive Era, most who have written about Smith's article have concluded that although he favored leaving colleges and universities to the market, he advocated tax-funded, state-run education for the earlier years, mainly to ensure the education of the poor.

I read Smith's thinking on schooling for the poor as more in line with his presumption of liberty in public policy. The evidence in support of a state interpretation is much less conclusive than commonly assumed, and the evidence for private and charity solutions is regularly overlooked. In the following, I trace the elements of the article which support my reading. For details and bibliography, I refer readers to research that pushes back against the pro-governmentalization reading (E. G. West 1964; 1980; 1990; 1994; Drylie 2016; 2020; 2021; Otteson 2023).

Who is "the publick?"

Smith observed that the poor could not afford the basics of education, and he felt deeply that they and civil society suffered. He thus writes:

> The publick can facilitate this acquisition [of the most essential parts of education] by establishing in every parish or district a little school, where children may be taught for a reward so moderate, that even a common labourer may afford it; the master being partly, but not wholly paid by the publick; because if he was wholly, or even principally paid by it, he would soon learn to neglect his business. (WN 785.55)

Smith undeniably calls for some sort of action in the article, but this passage cannot carry the weight that has regularly been placed upon it to establish Smith as a public education advocate (nor can any other). Smith does not prescribe an action—only stating what his agents "can" do. He also does not clearly specify who those agents might be—naming them as "the publick," which at the time was defined as "the people" (Ash, 1775) or "the body of mankind, or of a state or nation" (Johnson, 1768). While there has been little hesitation in scholarship to read the publick here as the state, in Smith's writing, the publick operates through either political mechanisms or voluntary structures of civil society. And in this case, both options, political and voluntary, do actually follow the above passage. He gives as examples of public action both a government-centered model (the Scottish parish system) and a voluntary association model (the charity system commonly associated with England). Smith is very likely merely positing options.

It would be wrong to infer an endorsement of governmentalization. Throughout the eighteenth century, many writers made observations about the poor similar to Smith's, wrote with similar sentiments, and made calls for action using similar language. Yet time and again what they sought was simply greater public spirit and public action, including better treatment of charities by government. No writer, to my knowledge, channeled a narrative of the troubles of the poor toward an end goal of financial support from government except for John Brown (to be discussed). Voluntary action seemed right for the task. Patience, not urgency, characterized the discourse. Neither "market failure" nor charity failure was conveyed.

It would have been out of sorts with this "Age of Benevolence" for Smith to wish to displace voluntary provision with state provision. He would have had to do some of the following: reject the voluntary charity movement as incapable, corrupt, or misdirected; quell the extant anxieties about the ideological influences of the state in education; dismiss the criticisms that the partially tax-based Scottish parish system was inept and corrupt; and disassociate public education from the much-maligned prior venture of the state into welfare (i.e., the Poor Laws). The future advocates for the state would feel compelled to make such arguments. Smith makes none.

Smith's final words on education

Beyond the historical context, Smith's official summary judgment of the issue of education funding poses problems for the standard readings which place government in the primary financial role. The judgment comes in a paragraph after the article, in the summary section called "The Conclusion of the Chapter." It jointly addresses the article on youth education and the article that follows on instruction for people of all ages, notably by religious institutions.

The paragraph consists of but two sentences. The first sentence is:

> The expence of the institutions for education and religious instruction, is likewise, no doubt, beneficial to the whole society, and may, therefore, without injustice, be defrayed by the general contribution of the whole society.

The second sentence is:

> This expence, however, might perhaps with equal propriety, and even with some advantage, be defrayed altogether by those who receive the immediate benefit of such education and instruction, or by the voluntary contribution of those who think they have occasion for either the one or the other. (WN 815.5)

The first sentence acknowledges that it might be proper for government to collect taxes for education. The second sentence, however, indicates that payments, which come "altogether" from students and charity, may demonstrate "equal propriety, and even some advantage." ("Voluntary contribution" was the definitive phrase for donation.) Thus, in the end, Smith points out that a more advantageous approach may be for government to not allocate a single cent of tax money toward education.

This final judgment has scarcely been acknowledged in scholarship, and worse, the inconvenient sentence has regularly been concealed (Drylie 2020). These final words, however, are a fair representation of the drift of the entire article about the education of youth—one which entertains a role for government but primarily informs us of what these "advantages" of private and voluntary affairs tend to be. To the entire article I now turn.

Smith's hypothesis and evidence on endowments

To begin the analysis, a word on the structure of Smith's argument is necessary. Many have noted that Smith discusses (in order) endowments, universities, ancient civilization, and the poor. But the *function* of this ordering is almost completely overlooked. The discussion of endowments offers a rigorous test of Smith's hypothesis concerning the incentive problems that attend publicly provided education. The discussion of universities defends his findings against casual dismissal. And the discussion of antiquity offers validation of his method of analysis. These earlier sections build an increasingly impervious criticism of government involvement. Attending to their function properly frames the fourth section about the poor.

The article begins by Smith establishing that private, voluntary action is the natural and proper course for education. Should one doubt it, Smith says, there is an alternative to evaluate: the "endowment" (as state-assured funding would similarly constitute). Smith proceeds to evaluate this alternative, and he offers a hypothesis: "The endowments of schools and colleges have necessarily diminished more or less the necessity of application in the teachers" (WN 760.5). Guaranteed salaries and their related protections, which flow from large endowments, diminish the incentive to serve students.

The pro-governmentalization interpretation has regularly claimed that the ensuing demonstration of the failing of endowments is confined to colleges and universities. Yet such scholars give—and can give—no evidence of Smith confining his criticism. The evidence runs to the contrary. First, Smith bases his hypothesis on a human tendency that applies to "every profession," and which by logical extension would include every sort of teaching profession (WN 759.4).

Second, Smith finds evidence across a wide spectrum of cases. Smith's evidence includes rich and poor universities, endowed grammar schools (what he calls "publick"), domestic tutors (what he calls "private"), unendowed schools for fencing, dancing and riding, and eventually also unendowed schools for young women. It is a matter of *fact*, then, to say that Smith examines both universities and non-universities. While universities receive the most criticism, they do so—in line with his hypothesis—because they have the largest endowments.

The case study of colleges and universities: outcomes v. intentions

The next section of the article picks up in paragraph 18, when Smith allows a counterargument to be voiced: "The parts of education which are commonly taught in universities, *it may, perhaps, be said*, are not very well taught. But had it not been for those institutions they would not have been taught at all" (WN 765.18, emphasis mine). In other words, something is better than nothing.

What follows is typically treated simply as an historical critique of universities. But it is also a critique of the above counterargument. Throughout, he makes clear that damage done to curricula is damage done to society at large. And the damage is pronounced. Something can be worse than nothing, much worse. He ends by pointing out the ironies of blind support for endowments. The better we endow universities, the worse they become (WN 772.34). And the worse they become, the more likely parents are to send their youth abroad which ends up ruining the character of youth even more (WN 773. 36). At least rhetorically, Smith appears willing to accept that the absence of universities would be better than this sort of something. Using the salient example of universities (which his audience worried about and had experience with), Smith creates a hard-hitting morality tale regarding naïve optimism.

A broader search for ancient examples: science v. testimony

In paragraph 38, Smith turns to the historical record of ancient civilizations to further test his theory. It is arguably a necessary turn. There was a tendency among potential readers to seek wisdom in the governance of ancient civilizations and to trust the histories as a source of truth over the more modern systematic (scientific) method which Smith was demonstrating.

Smith therefore examines the famous histories regarding gymnastics, music, a basic liberal education, philosophy and rhetoric, and law. In every case, he goes against the ancient historians and expends effort denying that the state had any positive and significant impact through funding. Then Smith goes further. He highlights the fallibility of historical narratives *as a method*. He asserts that the ancient historians erred because they were "predisposed" to celebrate ancient legislatures. He refuses their methods outright (WN 779.45).

The heart of this section occurs in a passage referencing Montesquieu. Smith writes,

> Notwithstanding, therefore, the very respectable authority of Plato, Aristotle, and Polybius, and notwithstanding the very ingenious reasons by which Mr. Montesquieu endeavors to support that authority, it seems probable that the musical education of the Greeks had no great effect in mending their morals, since, without any such education, those of the Romans were upon the whole superior. (WN 775-776.40)

Smith exclusively uses the term "ingenious" in *WN* with irony when applied to traditional authorities (Drylie 2023). This case is no exception.

Smith is rejecting Montesquieu's method of turning to these authorities for policy wisdom, and by extension he is rejecting what Montesquieu takes from them—faith in governmentalization of education (in *The Spirit of the Laws*, 1748). Montesquieu is a figure lost in modern historiographies of education, but in Smith's time he had provoked a heated (and frequently referenced) proxy debate specific to Britain. It was a debate between best-selling moralist John Brown who embraced Montesquieu's idea and prominent figure Joseph Priestley who opposed Brown (Brown 1765; Priestley 1765). This fleeting reference to Montesquieu—missed in modern scholarship to my knowledge—places Smith in the focal debate of his age, alongside Priestley as an opponent of governmentalization.

Paragraph 45 (the longest in the article) is the rightful conclusion of Smith's view of ancient civilization and of his overall position. Here he writes conclusively, "The demand for such instruction produced, what it *always* produces, the talent for giving it; and the emulation which an unrestrained competition *never* fails to excite, appears to have brought the talent to a very high degree of perfection" (emphasis mine). Demand begets supply; voluntary forces will *over time* provide; patience has merit over urgency. This sentence—which has all the natural harmony of the invisible hand in action—is the most absolute statement in an article that is otherwise carefully probabilistic. The market for education basically works like that for other goods.

His coda is a sequence of three ironies which again address the "something is better than nothing" sentiment: 1) Endowments not only corrupt schools, but also destroy private markets and thus the options for escaping endowed schools (WN 780.45); 2) if there were no endowed institutions, we would not have so many people foolish of everything practical and moral (WN 780.46); and 3) women, prohibited entry to such endowed schools, have been spared (WN 781.47). There can be no doubt where Smith stands regarding endowments and government funding of education.

Conclusion

Smith provides empirical evidence against state funding, rebukes lazy thoughts to the effect of "It can't hurt to try," rejects ancient writers who were predisposed to give the state credit, and takes sides in a fresh new debate, with Priestley against Montesquieu. The great strength of Smith's argument, however, leaves a riddle: Why would Smith not more forcefully reject governmentalization in schooling when it came to the poor?

The answer, to his credit, likely lies in him remaining true to his scientific approach. His hypothesis and results do not entirely preclude participation by government. Damage just moves "more or less" in proportion to the government's part (WN 759.4; 760.5, 760.6; 762.10; 780.45). Thus, a small government contribution would only do small damage to quality, utility, and the ability of charity markets as well as private ventures (of which there were many) to thrive. Small damage may be outweighed by the public and private good.

Still, the necessary smallness—and smallness does permeate his discussion of options—impacts how we should discuss this article. Government funding would in practice almost certainly merely *supplement* charity, not replace it (nor the fees, which he in any case insisted upon). The Scottish system had (by intention and in practice) served only such a supplemental role. And future reformers would continue to imagine building around, rather than replacing, charity. Thus, while Smith opens the door to government, it seems fair to think that he limits consideration to a tripartite tax-charity-fee model.

Nonetheless, in the end we must recognize that this *tax-charity-fee* model bears little resemblance to the modern public education system of today. Moreover, we must recognize that Smith expressly doubted even this limited, supplemental role for government in his final words on the topic—words which most scholars have elided.

My work has sought to encourage a sober reading of the article, rooted in what I have called the missing historiography of education (Drylie 2016, 2021). Aside from applications in the history of thought, this reading informs the question of how his views would translate to policy analysis today. One may be apt to suspect he would never place as much faith in charity and markets today. But Smith's article has the aperture in it which he could expand to see what would happen with increasing governmentalization. I venture to say that Smith would certainly approve of the broad public attention to education and the tendency toward local decision making, but still disapprove of the permanent and focal placement of government in this critical aspect of our lives.

References

Ash, John. 1775. *A New and Complete Dictionary of the English Language*. London: Edwin and Charles Dilly.

Bailey, Nathan. 1753. *An Universal Etymology of English Dictionary*. London: R. Ware.

Drylie, Scott. 2016. Interpreting Adam Smith's Views on the Education of the Poor in the Age of Benevolence. PhD diss., (George Mason University, 2016).

Drylie, Scott. 2020. Professional Scholarship from 1893 to 2020 on Adam Smith's Views on Schooling Funding: A Heterodox Examination. *Econ Journal Watch* 17(2): 350-391.

Drylie, Scott. 2021. Adam Smith on Schooling: A Classical Liberal Rereading. *Journal of Economic Behavior and Organization* 184: 748-770.

Drylie, Scott. 2023. Smith at 300: Men of Blessed and Beguiling Ingenuity. *Journal of the History of Economic Thought* 45(2): 226-228.

Johnson, Samuel. 1768. *A Dictionary of the English Language*. Dublin: W.G. Jones.

Otteson, James R. 2023. Adam Smith on Public Provision of Education. *Journal of the History of Economic Thought* 45(2), 229-248.

Smith, Adam. 1981 [1789]. An Inquiry into the Nature and Causes of the Wealth of Nations. Indianapolis: Liberty Fund.

West, E.G. 1964. Private Versus Public Education: A Classical Economic Dispute. *Journal of Political Economy* 72(5): 465–475.

West, E. G. 1980. Review of Adam Smith's Politics: An Essay in Historiographic Revision by Donald Winch. *Southern Economic Journal* 46(3): 997–999.

West, E.G. 1990. *Adam Smith and Modern Economics: From Market Behavior to Public Choice.* Aldershot: Edward Elgar.

West, E.G. 1994. Interview with Adam Smith. *The Region, Federal Reserve Bank of Minneapolis,* June 1.

CL Press

A Fraser Institute Project

https://clpress.net/

Professor Daniel Klein (George Mason University, Economics and Mercatus Center) and Dr. Erik Matson (Mercatus Center), directors of the Adam Smith Program at George Mason University, are the editors and directors of CL Press. CL stands at once for classical liberal and conservative liberal.

CL Press is a project of the Fraser Institute (Vancouver, Canada).

People:

Dan Klein and Erik Matson are the co-editors and executives of the imprint.

Jane Shaw Stroup is Editorial Advisor, doing especially copy-editing and text preparation.

Zachary Yost is Production Manager of CL Reprints.

Advisory Board:

Jordan Ballor, Center for Religion, Culture, and Democracy

Caroline Breashears, St. Lawrence Univ.

Donald Boudreaux, George Mason Univ.

Ross Emmett, Arizona State Univ.

Knud Haakonssen, Univ. of St. Andrews

Björn Hasselgren, Timbro, Uppsala Univ.

Karen Horn, Univ. of Erfurt

Jimena Hurtado, Univ. de los Andes

Nelson Lund, George Mason Univ.

Daniel Mahoney, Assumption Univ.

Deirdre N. McCloskey, Univ. of Illinois–Chicago

Thomas W. Merrill, American Univ.

James Otteson, Univ. of Notre Dame

Catherine R. Pakaluk, Catholic Univ. of America

Sandra Peart, Univ. of Richmond

Mario Rizzo, New York Univ.

Loren Rotner, Univ. of Austin

Marc Sidwell, New Culture Forum

Craig Smith, Univ. of Glasgow

Emily Skarbek, Brown Univ.

David Walsh, Catholic Univ. of America

Richard Whatmore, Univ. of St. Andrews

Barry Weingast, Stanford Univ.

Lawrence H. White, George Mason Univ.

Amy Willis, Liberty Fund

Bart Wilson, Chapman Univ.

Todd Zywicki, George Mason Univ.

Why start CL Press?

CL Press publishes good, low-priced work in intellectual history, political theory, political economy, and moral philosophy. More specifically, CL Press explores and advance discourse in the following areas:

- The intellectual history and meaning of liberalism.

- The relationship between liberalism and conservatism.

- The role of religion in disseminating liberal understandings and institutions including: humankind's ethical universalism, the moral equality of souls, the rule of law, religious liberty, the meaning and virtues of economic life.

- The relationship between religion and economic philosophy.

- The political, social, and economic philosophy of the Scottish Enlightenment, especially Adam Smith.

- The state of classically liberal ideas and policies across the world today.

www.ingramcontent.com/pod-product-compliance
Lightning Source LLC
Chambersburg PA
CBHW011833020426
42335CB00024B/2848